TRUTH BE TOLD

ALSO BY ETHAN HUNT:

LOST AND FOUND

FOR HIS GLORY

ETHAN HUNT

TRUTH BE

TOLD

EXPOSING THE LIE OF REJECTION AND
BUILDING A FOUNDATION OF TRUTH

CHRIST IS RISEN MINISTRIES

III

TRUTH BE TOLD

TRUTH BE TOLD

ISBN 978-1-542-50894-0

TEXT COPYRIGHT © ETHAN RAY HUNT

COVER PHOTO BY SHUTTERSTOCK.COM/ CARLOS E. SANTA MARIA

TRUTH BE TOLD: EXPOSING THE LIE OF REJECTION AND BUILDING A FOUNDATION OF TRUTH/ETHAN HUNT 1ST ED.

1. CHRISTIANITY 2. REJECTION 3. SELF HELP

PRINTED IN THE UNITED STATES OF AMERICA 2017

www.thecagelessmovement.com

NOW YOU'RE FEELING LOW.
WHAT THEY SAID WASN'T TRUE.
YOU'RE BEAUTIFUL. STICKS AND
STONES BREAK YOUR BONES. I
KNOW WHAT YOU'RE FEELING.
WORDS LIKE THOSE WON'T STEAL
YOUR GLOW. YOU'RE ONE IN A
MILLION. THIS IS FOR ALL THE
GIRLS AND BOYS ALL OVER THE
WORLD. WHATEVER YOU'VE BEEN
TOLD, YOU'RE WORTH MORE THAN
GOLD. SO HOLD YOUR HEAD UP
HIGH. IT'S YOUR TIME TO SHINE.
FROM THE INSIDE OUT IT SHOWS.
YOU'RE WORTH MORE THAN GOLD!

Britt Nicole

CONTENTS

DEDICATION

I want to dedicate this book to my wife Christine.
You've been by my side since the day I asked
you out. You've witnessed the transformation
I've made from when I first met you until now.
You're an eyewitness to God's healing touch on
my life. I know before the world began, He
planned you to be mine. You were my dream girl
before I ever met you and nothing could have
prepared me for the day you took my breath
away. You had the prettiest blue eyes and long
brown hair that cascaded past your shoulders.
Freckles adorned your face like the stars in the
night sky. You weren't prideful but respectfully
humble. You never tried to be someone you
weren't and that meant the world to me! Ever
since our dance, I couldn't stop thinking about
you and I'm so glad that you agreed to be the
mom to our beautiful children. You're a taste of
Heaven before the real thing and I honor you as
the priceless jewel that you are. Thank you for
being a part of my healing journey. You build me
up daily. You always know the right things to say
and your love for God amazes me. I love you,
Sweet Pea!

FORWARD

In your hands, you're holding a key to unlocking a revelation of God's heart for restoration. It has been a privilege knowing Ethan and watching the Lord bring restoration to his heart. God, through writing, is using Ethan to bring others into a place of truth where God can restore their lives.

We have a commission to disciple the nations. I believe the most powerful witness and discipleship starts in the home. The greatest and purest way to disciple the nations, is first through families. When parents exemplify Christ to their children, it gives them a solid foundation in Christ through an ever-changing world. It shouldn't surprise us, then, that the main attack of Satan is to destroy families and plant lies within our children. Many things we believe about ourselves are rooted back to our childhood. Some thoughts about ourselves are true, but some are lies. Lies about who we are (our identity) and lies about how God relates to

X

us (His identity), can be some of the most
devastating tools Satan will use. Not only are our
beliefs about ourselves formed early on, our
beliefs about God the Father also begin to be
determined at a young age. Our view of our
earthly father will many times carry over to our
view of our heavenly Father. Even when we have
godly parents that build us up in truth, Satan
comes to steal, kill and destroy. Understanding
the truth of who we are in God's eyes, and the
truth of who He is to us, however, can help keep
us grounded and not deceived. However, when
children are being raised without these truths,
Satan's lies can take root, and those lies often
times, carry on into adulthood. The lies impact
emotions and beliefs, and therefore begin to
impact relationships. As I've heard Ethan say,
"*hurt people hurt people*," meaning that those
who have been hurt in the past and are hurting
now, are likely to hurt those around them.
Beliefs, emotions, and the way we relate to the
world around us, are passed down to our
children. And when those are unhealthy beliefs,
emotions, and relations, we see a cycle that is
hard for the world to break.

Behold, I will send you Elijah the prophet before the coming of the great and dreadful day of the Lord. And he will turn the hearts of the fathers to the children, and the hearts of the children to their fathers, lest I come and strike the earth with a curse.

MALACHI 4:6

The good news is, it's not a cycle that the Lord can't break into. God is restoring the family units and bringing restoration to children. The last thing we see God say to the prophets in the Old Testament was concerning the restoration of families before He returns. He is releasing the Spirit of Elijah to turn hearts of the fathers back to their children and children's hearts back to their fathers. He stamped this passage with the urgency "*or else I will curse the land.*" If we don't respond to the movement of His Spirit, He will curse the land. We see Jesus and the disciples carry the same theme throughout the New Testament. Defining pure religion as one who

takes care of the fatherless (James 1:27).
Rebuking those who would hinder the children
from coming to Him (Matthew 19:14).

As I spend time with Ethan and read his
books, I see the spirit of Elijah upon his ministry.
The Lord is releasing him as a trumpet, not only
to reveal the injustice that is taking place in our
backyard, per se, but also a trumpet that God is a
tender Father that restores what the locusts have
eaten. We need those who will trumpet the
tender heart of the Father in this age. A clear call
that not only reveals who He is but how He feels
about His people. When we see God's heart for
His people, it creates two emotions within ours.
First healing, as we see God has not abandoned
us but draws near to the broken-hearted. Second,
we are called to love what He loves and take care
of the broken-hearted.

XIII

In this book, Ethan takes you through a journey of the loss in his life but then reveals hope, not just for him, but hope that Jesus gives to all, through restoration. To hear and see the transformation that has taken place in Ethan's life makes the truths of this book authentic and powerful. It is not another book with good ideas but it is a man's life who experienced the truths of the Word. When we read Ethan's journey, we understand that it can be our journey to a free heart. A heart that experiences freedom from bitterness. A heart that overcomes the fear of rejection. Most of all, a heart that experiences the love of our heavenly Father.

-Pastor Marc Hicks

NOTE TO READERS

This is a work of nonfiction. The events and experiences detailed herein are all true and have been faithfully rendered as remembered by the author, to the best of his ability. Some names have been changed in order to protect the privacy of individuals involved. All has been forgiven and forgotten between the author and the individuals mentioned.

RECOGNITIONS

First, I want to thank my Lord and Savior, Jesus Christ. You are so good to me and it overwhelms my soul. It's amazing that You have walked with me my whole life! Not one instant were you absent! Even though I didn't realize it then I realize it now. Thank You for giving me a shot at this thing called "life" and not giving up on me. I would have given up on myself a long time ago, but You didn't because You are faithful and I am so eternally grateful for this! I can't wait to worship You in person for eternity! You deserve all the praise forever and ever amen!

Second, I would like to thank the person who blew up on me. This book would not have been possible if I had not been pushed over the edge. Even though the experience hurt me tremendously, in a way, I guess I'm thankful that it did happen so that I can now help other people.

XVI

Next, I'd like to again thank my wife, Christine. You do so much for me! You help me when I'm going through the most difficult of circumstances. You are always ready to speak life to me and encourage me. You surely are my helper and I'm so thankful that I get to live and experience life with you!

I'd like to also recognize my pastor, Mark Hicks. It's amazing the people that God puts in our lives to help us make it to the finish line. Thank you for never sugar coating anything and being completely led by the Holy Spirit. My friendship with you strengthens me. You've helped me realize the "truth" in every situation.

†

XVII

Finally, I'd like to thank my editor, Sarah Hetherington. I remember when we first met. You were broken down and we stopped to give you a jump. We immediately hit it off as we realized that we were both believers. If I had a word to describe your impact on my life I'd have to say, "sister." That's who you've been in my life. Since meeting, you've always been an encouragement in my walk with God. I'm so thankful that the Lord put it on your heart to edit this book! You truly are a Godsend! Thank you for building up my "Godfidence!"

INTRODUCTION

I wrote another book, *Lost and Found.* In it, I described major events that highlighted both the worst times in my life and the best times in my life. It is untraditionally written, allowing the reader to finish it at a fast pace while giving the reader a sense of my creativity. The background for my life begins with my father returning from the Vietnam War. His job in the war was to clean up the dead bodies. To escape his daily horrors, he began to experiment with different drugs. Not only did he shock his body with the mixed drug concoction but he also understandably came down with Post Traumatic Stress Disorder. Leaving a wife at the airport in Vietnam, my father then found my mother and got her pregnant with two other boys before having me. My older brother was taken into the foster care system almost immediately after witnessed abuse but my other brother and I were not displaced. We were taken to my grandma's house to be raised away from the guidance of my mother. The house, in my eyes, became a place called, "The Dump of Sorrows." The trash piled high to the ceiling in that place and rats grew to call it home. Endless tortures took place there. We were beaten and starved. One of my father's favorite tortures was to cram my brother and I into a small dog cage in the dark basement. Fear was instilled within us at such a feeble age. It's all we ever knew. The abuse went on until I was seven. In a sudden turn of events, my brother worked up the courage to flag down the authorities. We were immediately placed into foster care where more abuse came and followed us into young adulthood. Worn and scarred, I turned to sex, drugs, material things, man-made religion, work, and education. Anything to drown out my inner screams. Nothing did though, until I met God in a bar. In a powerful surge of love, I completely repented of my sins and surrendered my life to Jesus. Forgiveness and self-worth followed. Now I walk out my destiny, bringing others with painful backgrounds like me, to the healing arms of their Savior!

"IF THE WORLD HATES YOU, KEEP IN MIND THAT IT HATED ME FIRST. IF YOU BELONGED TO THE WORLD, IT WOULD LOVE YOU AS ITS OWN. AS IT IS, YOU DO NOT BELONG TO THE WORLD, BUT I HAVE CHOSEN YOU OUT OF THE WORLD. THAT IS WHY THE WORLD HATES YOU."

-KING JESUS

CHRIST IS RISEN
MINISTRIES
PRESENTS......

TRUTH BE TOLD

XXIII

PART I: TRIALS

THE LAST STRAW

SOME PEOPLE ACCEPT AND CONFORM
TO THEIR WEAKNESSES IN LIFE.

I on the other hand refuse to conform. We were
made to be warriors and conquerors! The enemy
wants us to get comfortable even if it is
comfortable with being hurt. All the time! My
whole life I've faced countless rejections. It's
been beaten and engraved into the highways of
my brain that I am a nobody, worthless and
unusable. But you see, this is just a lie! The more
trials you face in life to break you down, the
stronger God's call is on your life!

Many have asked me, "*Will you continue to
write more books?*" At the time of this question,
I was never really looking forward to writing
another book because it was so much work to

write my first one. Writing a book is a big accomplishment in an ordinary world. I know how big it is. I've thought about it my whole life, my head stuck in books to escape my reality... My whole life I've been being trained to be an author and I never even realized it. From my tedious English classes to my typing classes. Back then, I thought it was just all a big waste of my time. "*What will I even use this stuff for in the real world?*" I thought to myself. God has surely opened the floodgates though! This is what I was made to do!

Still, even at this realization, it doesn't just erase the trauma I've experienced. I've still got a lot of healing to do. A lot of it! But I trust that God will bring me faithfully into His Kingdom. He will never give up on me. I am perfect in His sight, (flaws and all), because of the sacrifice that His Son Jesus Christ made for me. I am covered in His blood. It flows through my veins! I've learned that even though God could just completely heal someone, He usually will heal them in one area at a time. (So much patience is required!) Not only does this make me rely on Him in any circumstance but it also makes me appreciate each time He's brought me through something.

The reason I began this book is because of something that the enemy has been doing to me throughout my whole life and one day I had finally had enough!

I started a new job. I was promoted to Assistant Manager right away! And I thought that I had finally broken free from persecutions I'd faced in my past jobs. As a Christian, I kid you not, in every single job I've ever taken, I faced persecutions. I think in the spiritual world there is a target painted right on my back! Well, with this new job, I thought things were going so good and that I had finally made it. That is until the

owner of the business snapped on me. It came
out of nowhere! We had been getting along so
well. Everything was perfect. And then he just
snapped and let loose on me in front of all my
coworkers. Hurt instantly welled up deep inside
of me. It was as if he had taken a sword and
stabbed into my inner wounds of the past and
just kept on twisting it. It shocked me that it hurt
so bad. The enemy jumped right on board and
into my mind in that moment, "*You're
worthless!*", "*Nobody likes you!*", "*You're not
good enough!*", "*You're a loser!*" And in that
moment, I started to believe him. It was one of
my most painful work days ever. My whole day
turned gloomy and my inner self ached the rest
of the day and into the night. How had a stranger
made me so vulnerable? Why did I let his harsh
words penetrate my soul? I went home and fell
into a deep depression. The owner snapping on
me was the last straw for me. I could not take
one more strand of rejection. I didn't want to live
anymore. But in those moments, God taught me
something. He taught me to get back up because
He is with me. And He put in me the urge to
write this book to help others who may be going
through the same things. After that day, God
started a healing process in me to reverse my
rejections and show me my acceptance. He is so
good! He always takes a bad situation and uses it

for His glory! And this is how *Truth Be Told* began!

   Bear with each other and forgive one another if any of you has a grievance against someone. Forgive as the Lord forgave you.

COLOSSIANS 3:13

I WANT MY MOMMY

I NEVER KNEW IT WOULD HURT THIS BAD.

I guess I've been shoving it deep into the cavernous recesses of my mind for far too long. Her piercing and hateful words go through my mind from time to time, "*I wish I would have just aborted you!*" I feel as if there's a dam built behind my eyes and it's getting weak. It's just too much effort to hold these tears, this rejection and this pain in for much longer. But I'm supposed to be healed and restored and a strong, strong Christian. Sometimes I don't feel that way. I love the Lord, but subconsciously, I've built a wall. I know He's a good Father and He'd never hurt me but it's so hard to just let go and trust someone when I've been walked on my whole life. Rejection after rejection. Insult after insult. Sometimes I wish I could just shut off my brain and emotions and become a robot. It's hard to carry all of this. I was never meant to. Jesus said, "*Cast your burdens on Me.*" If I love Him so much then why is it so hard to obey and trust

Him? I have a deep longing for a loving mother and father. Even though I'm a dad myself, I feel as if I've missed out. I've even been so desperate as to ask other grown adults to be my "new" father and mother. I know what you're thinking, "*Awkward!*" and yes, you're right, it is! God knew what He was doing when He created the family unit. He knew each child needed a loving father and mother. Someone to nurture and speak life into them. Someone to love them unconditionally throughout life's toughest trials. I don't have that and I feel like I've been left out. It sucks. I so desperately needed that affirmation, that affection. When the pain comes, I cover it up as quickly as possible. I don't want to face my past. I want to make it all just go away. At times, I feel like a child again. Sometimes when my wife hugs me and holds me close, I daydream I'm a little boy being snuggled by his momma. It might sound weird, but it's kind of comforting in a strange way. It's a craving that never seems to go away.

I remember as a child newly accepted into foster care, finding out that my mom could have kept me but chose not to. It stung bad to find that out. I was surrounded by the new toys she had purchased for me as farewell gifts. These toys meant nothing but deep hurt and memories.

On our last visit with our mom, my brother and I were taken to the city mall. We could buy anything we wanted! Anything! We found a lot of cool toys. It was weird though. I would have rather had my family than all of these toys. Deep down I knew that this was the last time I'd see her. Everyone acted like everything was okay though so I went along with it. We took a lot of pictures and went shop to shop. We ate together. I didn't know what my older brother was feeling, but I was being tortured on the inside. *"Why couldn't time stand still to let me have more time with my mommy? Couldn't she in the spur of a moment decide she wanted me? How could everyone smile and act so happy?"* These thoughts swirled around my little mind like a violent hurricane. The storm of the century was going on inside me and no one even seemed to notice. No one knew the deep sting of rejection that was being planted in me that day. Our day at the mall was coming to an end. My mom held my hand in hers and we all walked out with bags and bags of toys. The closer we got to the vehicle, the worse I began to feel. I felt sick to my stomach. Finally, the worst thing happened. My mom told us that this was the last of our visitations. This was our last moment with her. I can barely describe the feelings I felt that day. My soul was crushed. Despair and depression enveloped me, wrapping me up and holding me closer than my mom ever had. I couldn't wrap my mind around it. It was almost like being at a funeral. I didn't want to be adopted, I wanted my own mom. I didn't want to live with strangers who always yelled at me and told me what a bad little boy I was. My father had already beaten that into me in my first six years of life! It was such a dark and nightmarish day. My mom didn't want me. That's one of the worst rejections anyone on earth can ever face. Your own flesh and blood turning their back on you. It's intense so intense that as a little six-year-old boy, I didn't want to live anymore. Luckily, I didn't know how to end it all or maybe I would have. I can still feel the pain of that day as I type this. Tears well up behind my eyes, but I won't let them escape. I can't yet. I don't want my wife and children to see me like this. I'm not to that point in my journey yet.

My whole life I never realized the pain of that day because I shut those feelings and emotions off. I hid them, never expecting them to pop out again like some sick and twisted jack-in-the-box. But here they are. Like dirty laundry that's been stuffed in the closet. The same pain. The same emotions heaped in my lap. Recently, I watched a program on *Sid Roth's It's Supernatural.* The whole episode was about the "rejection spirit" and how it can even enter the baby in its mother's womb if the mom doesn't want it. This all began to make sense to me. The program spoke of how the demon will draw people to you that it knows will reject you, causing a pattern and instances of rejection throughout your whole life. It all began to make sense. My life was peppered with so many instances of rejection. They played through my mind like a movie. This happened so much to me that I really began to believe that I was worthless. My whole life I've never had any

self-worth, and when I began to get some,
something would happen to snatch it away from
me. The devil certainly doesn't play fair!

When I first became a believer, I thought
things would be perfect, and for a while they
were. But some things crept back in again. Or
maybe they had never left. Maybe my encounter
with God had blinded me to my problems for an
instance. I want to help others but how can I help
heal others when I'm not completely healed
myself? I don't want to be one of those phony,
hypocritical Christians. I want to be a real Christ
follower. I want to be real, genuine, and loving,
just like Jesus was. I need inner healing that only
He can give me. I've pleaded with Him
repeatedly to just heal me. It'd be fantastic for all
my inner wounds to be healed in a flash like the
stories in the Bible. I'm starting to learn that
more often, healing happens step by step. God
will continuously heal you, layer by layer. The
pain hurts worse than physical pain. My spirit is
so bruised and battered. It's so hard for me to
think that I'm accepted, that Jesus died

personally just for me. How could anyone love me like that? But I know He did and He does. I just know it!

I believe all this pain that I'm allowing to resurface is part of the healing process. The Lord is answering my prayers. I'm in surgery right now. I need to trust the Master Surgeon. He made me and knows what makes me tick. He loves to heal and answer prayers. It brings great joy to Him. I trust and love Him so much! It seems too good to be true but I know we'll have a happy ending. One day all these pains and tears will be gone forever!

It's been a long hard journey. I know there's hope. Even though this world is like hell sometimes, other times it's got pieces of heaven hidden in it. You just need to be willing to search for them. I know it's hard to break that inner wall that you've built up in defense so you won't have to feel pain again. But trust me from experience, hiding behind a wall only brings more hurt and loneliness. That's why it is so critical to forgive. Each time we choose not to we are adding another brick to our inner wall. Each time we choose to forgive, like Jesus did, we are smashing the walls, one brick at a time! Just like the walls of Jericho, your wall will soon come tumbling down!

Though my father and mother forsake me, the Lord will receive me.

PSALM 27:10

ALICE & GENE

In FOSTER CARE, THERE WAS NEVER ANY STABILITY.

I was quickly learning that rejection came in many forms. Although not exactly rejection, the night that I was taken away from my father felt just as bad.

It was the night before Thanksgiving. My brother and I were in the house watching *Fox Kids* and our father was out tending to a fire in the front yard. In his boredom with what the T.V. was offering, my brother crept outside. I didn't think anything of it until a heard a "*WHOOSH!*" I looked out the living room window to see tongues of flames leaping about wildly. I ran out in panic to find my father in order to tell him. As I gave him the information we realized that my brother was nowhere in sight. He started to fearfully yell my brother's name but he never answered. I was instructed to load up into the vehicle while my father put out the fire.

We drove for what seemed like hours scouring the dark, misty streets. We also combed all the local grocery stores. Frantic, yet defeated, we pulled back up to the house which was now filled with the flashing red and blue lights of police cruisers. My father instructed me to hide and be quiet in a sleeping bag that was in the car. He got out but never returned. That's when fear took over. A few minutes later, I peeked out to see an officer approaching my side of the car. Time stopped and my heart leaped to my throat. The officer opened my door and told me to follow him to his car.

Any time my grandmother was mad at us, she would tell us that she would call the cops and have us hauled off to jail. This instilled such fear in me and my brother that we'd often resort to hiding out of sight for the rest of the day. So, as I was interacting with the police this day, you can only imagine how scared I was!

The officer opened his cruiser door and I was sat right next to my brother. Fear hit me like a freight train and panic swept through me like a tidal wave. My whole world was flipped over in a matter of minutes. It was all too much for me to handle and I completely lost it, crying uncontrollably. My brother asked the police officers if they'd go get my favorite teddy bear, Baby Nie-Nie, and they did. This comforted me to a certain level.

We pulled away as my father was being placed
in handcuffs. I couldn't understand or
comprehend why they were doing this to him. I
thought that cops were my enemies. At least
that's what my father and grandmother had told
me my whole life.

As we drove along, the officers showed us the
different aspects of their vehicle. These included
the spotlight, the siren, and the radio. I began to
trust them a little. But as I fully put my trust in
them, we pulled up to an enormous log home.
One of the officers went up to the door and a
woman with short blonde hair came out. After
explaining that my brother and I would be
staying with her and her husband for a while, we
were escorted up and into their expansive home.
I was amazed at the beauty of the amazing
architecture, but my fear crippled me too
intensely to be able to enjoy it. After finally giving
my trust over to the officers, they had to leave.
They hugged us and gave us teddy bears and
then just as suddenly as they appeared in our life,
they were gone.

✝

A bubble bath was immediately made ready for us as soon as the officers left. Lots of toys were dumped in. I was so confused and heartbroken but at least I had my brother by my side.

✝

After being cleaned up, we were dried off and put in unfamiliar clothes and into unfamiliar beds. I prayed that night that God would please help us. I was so scared. As we awoke in the morning, the smell of Thanksgiving was heavy throughout the air. The smell, although it smelled good, frightened me because my father had always taught me to only eat food that was kosher, food that was specially blessed by a rabbi. We sat around the table adorned with holiday trimmings but I could not muster one single bite. My brother on the other hand, gobbled down his entire plate. He was rewarded with desert and freedom to do whatever he wanted. I didn't get

19

anything and was sent to my new room. I was devastated and cried bitterly in my room. I didn't understand any of the confusion that was going on around me. I just wanted my father back.

Eventually, due to our new foster parent's hectic schedules, we were enrolled in daycare. It was a nightmare all over again for me. It was on a traditional farm with a big red barn and corn fields. The only thing that really enticed me about coming here was the fact that we'd get to play video games for as long as we wanted. Other than that, each day was complete and utter torture for me as uncertainty wrung out my soul like a wet sponge. I was a stranger in a strange land and it was all too much for me to handle at my delicate age.

One day, all of us daycare kids were outside playing. It was a sunny, cloudless day and manure was fresh on the air. All of a sudden, my brother strips butt naked and starts running through the corn field. All of us burst out laughing as we tried to catch up with him. My brother was a hoot, that was for sure! All of our fun and games ended when our foster mom picked us up though. As soon as we arrived home, she was on the phone right away. Hours later, someone picked up my brother. Fear gripped my soul and my tears flowed unceasingly.

Every night, through many tears and pleading, I prayed to God to bring my brother back. It was like a piece of me was torn from my own body. I didn't know how much I really loved him till he was completely erased from my life. Every waking morning was another reminder that he was gone. The only thing I could manage to choke down was fish sticks and fries. This was all I would eat, 24/7. My foster mom tried numerous things to get my mind off him;

watching movies, playing computer games, going outside. Nothing worked. In what seemed like an eternity, I was finally graced with the option to go visit my brother at the Department of Human Services. I was so relieved! Every minute in my brother's presence was like pure gold to me! I remember always begging his new parents for me to be able to go home with them. It was such a tragic scene! I would beg and whimper and try everything thing in my power to stay with my brother but nothing ever worked. I began to slip lower and lower into a depression that a child should never have to endure.

Growing up in my father's care, all the gifts anyone would ever give us, he'd keep and return them back to the store for the money. Each time he'd do this, a chunk would be ripped out of my heart. It's hard to explain, but it was as if every toy that was taken away from me was a part of my childhood being sold off. Eventually, Christmas rolled around. My depression eased off for a little while as I gazed at my presents. There were so many! One especially caught my attention though. It was so big, it towered above my head! I couldn't believe it! I was so excited! The little joy I found would soon be gone though.

✝

Close to Christmas, my foster mom told me that I would be staying with one of her friends for a little while. We packed all of my stuff into her car and were off. (Back then, being naïve, it never dawned on me that I was being transferred.) We went on for a distance in complete silence. I sensed that something was wrong and immediately slipped behind my inner defenses like a snail in its shell. We went further and further into the country finally arriving at a trailer surrounded by an expansive horse farm. Not much was said. My stuff was unloaded and the person I had begun to open up to was gone just like that. The syringe of rejection pierced my veins once again and flooded my being with the complete persona of abandonment. I was orphan Ethan. Nobody wanted me. I was tossed around to and froe like a ragdoll. I couldn't understand why nobody loved me.

✝

Each event that occurred like this in my childhood drove me deeper and deeper into solitary confinement. Like I said earlier, if I would have known a way to end my life, I would have! I was a child, new to the world and I wanted to end my own life. This world is so messed up! No child should ever have to ponder something like this! Maybe you can relate with me or maybe you can't. But the devil was using me as fertile ground for his plans of destruction at an early age. He planted so many crops within me! He thought he was going to yield a harvest but he was so wrong! With such a vast emptiness in me, hope always seemed like a fantasy growing up. I didn't believe in hope. I didn't believe in joy or peace or love. All those words were fictitious to me. Lies made up to make people feel better. That's all they were to me. I couldn't understand why God would even make me. I didn't know it at the time but my future would hold vast amounts of joy that I couldn't ever have imagined in my wildest dreams!

For I know the plans I have for you, plans to prosper you and not to harm you, plans to give you hope and a future.

JEREMIAH 29:11

SCHOOL BLUES

Have you ever gotten the school blues before?

You know, you do something bad and get scolded by the teacher. Well this takes me to one of my first episodes of rejection in school.

When living with my birth dad, he would never allow us to go to public school in fear that we might touch pork or get brainwashed or something. (He followed the Jewish Laws) I do have fond memories of homeschooling. It wasn't all bad. I was comforted by my father's masculinity as he read to me and taught me. I still remember the smell of the work book pages and that there were pictures of ducks throughout. I do believe I learned addition and subtraction through his methods so I can't complain too much. One day, near Christmas, *The Adams Family movie* was playing in the background and you could hear the steady hum of the space heater and feel it's life sustaining warmth. I remember *Pillsbury Dough Boy* commercials coming on. I loved watching his little belly get poked and watching his cute countenance as he giggled. Other Christmas commercials were coming on as well. It was such a memorable day for me as I sat and did my schoolwork, watching out the window as a school bus dropped off other children. From what my father told me, I was very intimidated by the public-school system and never wanted to go there. So, it was much to my surprise and horror when my new foster family enrolled me in 1st grade.

The school was called Cherry Street Elementary. I'd always ride in a van full of other children to school and it was very uncomfortable for me. We'd get to school a little early so we'd get to play on the playground for a while. Other kids would ask me my age and they never believed me that I was a year older than them.

Physically I was supposed to be in second grade but at least I got to skip Kindergarten! My brother on the other hand got to go straight to 3rd grade! I always felt like he was lucky and that it was no fair!

It was all so new to me. Having my own desk, being around so many other children. I kind of started to like it.

One day, we were all huddled around for story time on the carpet. One very enthusiastic kid was determined for me, the new kid, to become his new friend. He kept talking and talking to me. I was trying to listen to the story but this kid wouldn't stop talking to me! I wanted to be friendly and liked but I knew I needed to be quiet at such a time as this. Eventually the teacher looked over to see what looked like a

28

conversation between us. She looked directly into my eyes, face beat red, and screamed, *"ETHAN! GO SIT AT YOUR DESK, AWAY FROM EVERYONE ELSE!!!!!!!"* I hung my head, so ashamed and embarrassed. My face felt like it had caught on fire and turned a brilliant shade of scarlet. Immediately thoughts of worthlessness poured through my mind and soul. I believed, (even though I hadn't uttered one peep), that I was guilty and that I belonged away from my other classmates, that I was a total and complete reject.

It was like a virus that consumed me. It started with small incidents, and somehow, just somehow, it always connected me with the "right" person who would more than gladly take me down another notch. It chipped at me as it got heavier and heavier upon my soul, draining my personality.

A few weeks later, I brought my pet caterpillars to school. I had made them a house out of a shoe box and even made them little furniture! I was so excited to show all my classmates! I showed each one of them, even the teacher. Recess came so we all poured outside. I was the first to come back in. I found my little companions squished all over the place! I was heartbroken! Who would do such a thing? Another wave of rejection passed over me. It hit me like a ton of bricks! Two down, one more to go!

The 1st grade at Cherry Street Elementary had a tradition. Every year they'd put on a circus assembly for the whole school. The children got to pick their own characters and costumes. I wanted to be the gorilla. The costume caught my attention right away. It was furry and realistic looking; the only problem was that I was far too small to fit into it. Disappointed but not discouraged, I chose to be a strong man instead.

All I had to do for this position was make a pair of weights using tinfoil and show off my muscles. Piece of cake! The next day, the assembly started. The bleachers were filled with 2nd and 3rd graders. I was proud of my costume and prop. The real kicker too was that I had found the perfect way to look like I was really lifting real weights! I would grunt and push all the blood to my face, making my veins pop out. I thought I was doing such a great job until I heard, "*FAKE! YOU'RE A FAKE!*" being shouted at me from the bleachers. The older kids kept taunting me and making fun of my effort. I felt humiliated and wanted to go back to my classroom immediately. I never knew that school would be so hard. I thought everybody would be friends.

The enemy kept pursuing me. He kept washing me in "worthlessness." Even up until today I am still battling these lies. They've formed a highway in my brain. It's rooted very deeply! But I believe the Lord is so much more powerful than these lies that I've believed my entire life! I was created for a purpose! I'm not a mistake! I have a destiny!

Maybe you're reading this and can fully understand and identify with me, maybe you can't but you know somebody that can. The enemy is so good at being bad! After all, he's been doing this for thousands of years! He's studied every man and woman throughout the entire age of humanity. Society may change, but human nature does not. But there is hope! We are not alone. Scripture says Jesus was tempted with every sin known to man. So, everything you're going through, He's been through and made it! He has defeated the grave and now He stands ready to raise us from the dead! He is good! Pure goodness flows through Him. He has a future and a hope for you and He wants to shield you from your oppressors here and now, in the physical and the spiritual realms. It's time we stand up and walk in the destiny that we were created for! It's time to be strong in the Lord, my friend! No matter what flies into our lives, we already have victory in Jesus!

Surely God is my help; the Lord is the one who sustains me.

PSALM 54:4

FAMILY MATTERS

A SENSE OF BELONGING IS ALL I EVER CRAVED.

But I wouldn't feel that for almost thirty years. After going through the drama of floating through the foster care system, it was extremely riveting to be plopped down at my adoption home. New place after new place engraved in me the sense of never being safe in one place. Upon arrival at my new and final home, I got in to trouble quickly. But that was like heaven compared to what this place had in store for me in the future. Everything started off relatively calm. There was a functioning family unit. I had my own belonging. In the beginning, everything was bearable. Still scary, but bearable.

My new family had a large brown house that was built on a lake. The front yard was full of green grass, a big oak tree, and decorative shrubs. The back porch gave way to a beautiful pathway that traveled past an old shed, a sandbox, a trampoline, a wooden swing, and finally on to the lake itself. On numerous occasions, swans and ducks could be seen swimming through the cattails. It was a very wonderful place to try and grow up as a kid. I knew on the inside I was really hurt but realized that I might be okay at this place.

Most of the time, my new parents were friendly. Especially when trying to get me to agree to let them adopt me. They promised me that I could pick a new name, a restaurant of my choice to celebrate, and a marvelous trip around the country to see Las Vegas, the Grand Canyon, Mount Rushmore, Yellowstone, and other worthy sites. It all sounded so good to me so I agreed. (I don't know why they really even needed me to agree...)

The day of our adoption approached quickly. My brother and I dressed as sharp as young men could dress. Then we whisked away to the court house. The proceedings went fast and smooth Soon we both had a new last name. For our celebration restaurant, we chose *Ponderosa*, a steakhouse known for its endless buffet. We stuffed ourselves full of tasty morsels and then finished off the night with big bowls of ice cream. And that was that. We were officially adopted. All seemed well.

†

Our new family unit now consisted of both our adopted parents, six brothers, and two loving dogs. I always looked up to the older boys who were about sixteen. My favorite always wrestled with us on the trampoline pretending we were in the *WWE*. Also, he'd synchronize football and basketball games. I never had that positive role

model to look up to until I met him. He always
kept us active. The other one was quieter and
laid back. He often took our youngest brother up
to his room and fed him ice cream. Later we
found out that he was trying to groom him by
showing him X-rated magazines. We didn't find
out until he and our adopted dad got in a fight
and he ended up moving out and molesting a
boy and a girl down the street. Then my younger
brother spilled the beans about what had been
going on.

Soon both older brothers were gone and things
began to change. Our adopted dad began to get
gruffer and more ornery. He began telling our
adopted mom to start being tougher on us and to
quit showing favoritism. Soon she became mean
too, for reasons unknown, wrestling us down to
the floor when we got in trouble and sitting on
our chest. Our adopted father always seemed
like he was getting satisfaction out of it.

Everything around us started to change rapidly. Before we knew it, our beloved home was sold and we moved to a brand-new house out in the country. This is when things took a change for the worse!

The first thing that happened was that all of our toys were stripped from us, boxed up, and put in the pole barn. (Mind you, most of us were eight and nine. Inside it feels like I never even had a childhood!) Then they started giving us heavy writing punishments. Soon after, our food intake went down and physical abuse began. It cut me deeply to go through more abuse. I had gone through so much and instead of healing, I was repeating the cycle again. At family events, we were pushed aside like we were nobodies We often had to clean the house until it was spotless. Then, we could no longer eat at the table with the "real" family but had to sit in the basement and eat alone. Rejection yet again hit me straight between my eyes. My life went something like this: school, chores, sentences, outside; school, chores, sentences, outside; school, chores, sentences, outside, etc. That was it. It was an endless cycle of living a mundane existence. I didn't feel special. I didn't know what my purpose here on earth was. All I believed is that I was a mistake that happened to grace the face of planet earth.

It hurt a lot, probably worse than physical pain. Just the gnawing pain of not belonging, not having a family. I felt like an orphan and that all my adopted parents were in it for was the pay check. I was just a pay check! They didn't want me because they loved me. They wanted me because I was literally money! When they looked at me, maybe all they really saw were dollar signs. It was this worthless feeling of being used that made me begin to question my own existence.

I was blind to the love of God at that point. I didn't realize that I in fact belonged to a much bigger heavenly family. His is a close-knit family that spans the entire earth! A family from every tribe, tongue, and nation! A great multitude that no man can number! A family so intertwined and interconnected that the human mind can't even comprehend it! God loves His family! We are His sons and daughters and He made us to expand His family to even greater dimensions!

Without accepting and believing the truth, we begin to plummet into a downward spiral that ultimately leads to our death. We begin to hate ourselves. We begin to stew in depressing anger and hopelessness. This was not the intended plan! The whole earth is under the dark spell of sin. Hope, in this world is usually nothing more than a myth. Without God, people are walking without love because God is love. Without God, there is no healing but only, deep, deep cruelty and hurt. Jesus is the ONLY way! In the Kingdom that our Lord is bringing, these things will no longer be so! They will not even be a distant memory! For eternity, we'll soak in love and we'll fellowship as one big happy family!

Therefore, since we are surrounded by such a great cloud of witnesses, let us throw off everything that hinders and the sin that so easily entangles. And let us run with perseverance the race marked out for us.

HEBREWS 12:1

CHESTER

I'M SURE A LOT OF US HAVE
EMBARRASSING PASTS THAT HAVE
ALWAYS DEFINED US.

I brought this difficult time in my life up in my
last book but I want to go into more detail
because it has really caused a lot of damage to
my self-confidence. Out of everything, this is the
one incident that opened up vast amounts of
false shame in my heart. It's hard to talk about
but I know how important it is to bring the
darkness to the light.

   A few months after I moved in with my
adopted family, a startling reoccurring cycle
began in my life.

It began one morning as I was getting ready for school. I heard from my adopted father's bedroom, "*Say that Ethan touched you and I'll give you a bag of candy.*" It shocked me to my core and fear cascaded on me like Niagara Falls. All throughout my school day, and on my bus ride to and from school, those words swirled violently around and around inside my head.

As soon as I walked through the door, the atmosphere of fear intensified and finally I was immersed in the worst way imaginable.

My adopted niece's parents were there waiting for me, arms crossed and furious. All my siblings gathered around, knowing that something was about to go down. I was surrounded and there was no place I could run or hide. This was it for me. I felt like Daniel in the lion's den.

Both my adopted father and his son began accusing me of grotesque sexual sins, things I have never even heard of or even knew of at my age. Relentlessly, hatred and rage battered against my soul and broke through to the shattered boy within me. So many voices sounded and so much yelling took place. The room was in complete chaos. Every ounce of confidence I once held was gone. Humiliation assaulted me from every side. It wrecked and destroyed me.

Her father grabbed me and pulled me out the door without a coat. I was drug through the snow to the lake. I was picked up by the throat and threatened that I'd be drowned in the lake if I ever touched his daughter again.

✝

It completely devastated my childhood and destroyed me from the inside out.

✝

Years went by, and once and awhile I'd be taunted and reminded of this sick accusation, bringing on new layers of shame each time.

✝

Eventually, it just became part of me and I began to hate myself. Subconsciously, I labeled myself a "creep". I was so angry at myself for nothing. Each day, new levels of self-hatred exploded deep within me. My self-hatred drove me to isolate myself from others. I didn't feel worthy to have friends so I made sure never to get close to anyone again in fear that something bad might happen to me.

When I finally became a teenager, my adopted parent's daughter took me down to her house in Detroit to spend a few weeks. I had no clue what other shame would be dumped on me.

Since elementary, I kept a journal. Being a teenager and all, I wrote about girls a lot. And I mean a lot! My nephew found it and put it in his sister's bedroom. When their parents found out I was completely ostracized. It felt like a cannonball hit me right in the gut. Fear, depression, guilt, shame, and hate filled me up from my head to my toes. I was kicked out of

their house and dropped off with one of my
parent's friends. I was instantly labeled, "Chester
the Molester", and would daily be taunted about
it. At that point, I was dead on the inside. So
much pain surfaced and I didn't want to live
anymore. It was God that kept me from hurting
myself. I so badly wanted to end everything right
then and there. I can't even begin to explain the
season of torment and pain I went through. It
was all on the inside. I was already a loner.
Instead of building me up from my years of
abuse, I was torn down, and brought lower than
when I first began. The weight was real. The
heaviness was like cement.

   The devil tried to mold me into a person I was
not in my youth. He's a liar. Maybe you've been
labeled and told something so much that you
begin to believe it throughout your life. It's not
true! God created you for Him. It's because of
Him that your alive right now and He loves you
so very much! He wants to heal you from the
past lies in your life, ripping them out by the
roots. Your past circumstances don't define you!

God does and it's when you let go and run to His
arms that He's able to calm your stormy past!

God will fight the battle for you.

EXODUS 14:14

KISS ME

CAN YOU REMEMBER WHEN YOU HAD YOUR FIRST CRUSH?

I can. And it wasn't pretty. I used to think that if you stared at a girl for long enough, then she'd know how much you really liked her. (I know, creeper!) I hadn't cared much for girls besides having a major crush on my 3rd grade teacher, Ms. Bauer. I really wanted to marry her! Anyways, I hit 4th grade and right away my eyes landed on the fairest, most beautiful girl in the class. She was taller than the rest of the girls and what really got my attention was her long blonde hair and sparkling blue eyes. I didn't understand the rush of feelings I felt when I was around her. I couldn't stop thinking about her. She literally took my breath away. It seems like I was born a hopeless romantic. (Looking back, I once thought that a girl could heal all my past rejections!) Remembering all the stuff I put that poor girl through makes me grit my teeth now. I was so cheesy! I don't know how many times I asked her to be my girlfriend. One day, after

listening to some old sappy love songs, I decided
that I wanted to serenade her on the playground.
I told my friend to go get her and meet me by a
tree. I was going full throttle with the idea. I
thought for sure I'd sweep her off her feet. The
lyrics to the song I was going to sing to her were,
"*Two divided by one, would only be one, and
one is a lonely number...*" I finally chickened out
and called it off. I am so glad I did!

  Another time that I actually did go through
with one of my love-sick plans was on Valentine's
Day. We all had our own homemade card
envelopes hanging off the white boards. I made
sure to make her the biggest heart shaped card
and write the most romantic things I possibly
knew at the time. I'm sure it was horrific. I
slipped my masterpiece into her envelope when
no one was looking. Soon, all the girls were
hovering over my crush's shoulders reading every
word that I had written. I thought I had hit a
grand slam but was confused when she rushed
out of the room, her face fire truck red. I was

starting to get used to rejection. At that time, I would have rejected myself too!

✝

I never did win over my crush's heart but my curiosity for girls never vanished. It grew. At my adopted home, I was surrounded by five other brothers. Most of us were going through puberty at the same time. Let's just say another girl in the family took full advantage of this. She was about 19 and most of us were below the age of 15. She'd take us on long walks and our adopted parents trusted her. She taught us boys all about the birds and the bees. I'm pretty sure we all would have passed sex ed. with flying colors after our conversations with her. We all were head over heels for her. Every walk was another intense and fascinating lesson. One day, while back in the woods, she got the idea that we would play Truth or Dare. We definitely crossed lines into the land of inappropriate as we competed to see who could get the farthest with her. Things started to get raunchy. It was finally my turn to pick truth or dare and I chose dare. My brothers dared me to make out with her. I did. I saw fireworks. In my excitement, I ended up telling one of my other brothers who wasn't there that day. He told my parents. Things got ugly. Not for her, but for me. They talked with her and decided that they believed her over me. She said that I completely fabricated the whole ordeal. My parents decided that yet again, I was some sick, perverted, and twisted boy. I was told that I was never allowed to go on any more walks and I was grounded. It felt horrible. I felt so betrayed and yet again, that "R" word again, **REJECTED**. I was miserable. More worthless lies were piled into my mind by our enemy, the devil.

Whatever rejection you've faced in your life, God wants to heal you from it! See, the devil uses people who aren't saved, as puppets, to do his bidding. It's not actually that person that has rejected you, but Satan! God accepts you though! It doesn't matter what wrong you've done in life. If you'll repent and accept that you were in the wrong, He'll wipe your slate clean and remember your transgressions no more! God is so merciful that if Hitler would have repented of his war crimes he would have been completely forgiven! I know this from looking at the life of Paul in scripture. He was one of the ultimate killers of Christians in that time yet God forgave him and used him to write most of the New Testament. If God can forgive both of them, then He can surely forgive you of anything you have ever done! What a great God we serve! He is so mighty! He wants a good life for you here on earth and in the life to come! Bad circumstances may happen, but don't let them define you! Don't let them control you! God has made it very clear in His Word how He feels about you! You are His child and He is your Father. He loves you so very much! You are the King's child! You belong to Him! Spend time to get to know Him and you'll see that I am right. You are His. Nobody and nothing can ever take that away from you! He's always accepted you. Will you accept Him as your one and only? In our rejection, sometimes we make it a habit to reject others, as well as our Creator, even if we don't truly mean to. Coming close to God is the only way to heal!

Flee the evil desires of youth and pursue righteousness, faith, love and peace, along with those who call on the Lord out of a pure heart.

2 TIMOTHY 2:22

FIELD TRIP

A LOT OF CRUELTY CAN TAKE PLACE
AT THE HANDS OF CLASSMATES.

I have a lot of fond memories of my two years of
elementary school under Mrs. Bower. (Not Ms.
Bauer, my third-grade crush, but Mrs. Bower,
who happened to be at a different school and
taught a different grade. Same pronunciation
though. My new teacher would end up being my
all-time favorite teacher.) At first, I wasn't thrilled
about my move from the suburbs to the country.
I played it cool going into 4th grade. I tried hard
to not show how nervous I really was to be the
new kid at school again. To me, it was just
another adventure. My first day of class consisted
of watching videos about the mining of iron ore.
The previous night, I hadn't gotten any sleep
because of my excitement for my 1st day of
school. I kept nodding off in class and decided to
head to the restroom and even fell asleep while
in there!

Days passed and I grew accustomed to my new school.

I got into the groove of getting good grades. In fact, I really enjoyed the sensation of successfully completing assignments while putting my all into them. I also picked up reading. Books became one of my ways to escape.

There was such a sense of unity in my class. We were family. It wasn't long before I found my niche within the class. I became the class clown and I loved every minute of it! I didn't find my place completely until a certain project took place.

We had just successfully completed a book and our assignment was to act out or make a diorama of the book. Lots of classmates choose the first option. I had no idea what I would do until a classmate submitted a recording of himself acting out a scene. It got the whole class laughing and that's when a light bulb came on in my head. I knew I wanted to do the same thing but get the class into an even bigger uproar!

I decided to make wigs. Instead of playing a recording, I was actually going to act out the scene myself, playing each of the characters! I asked my teacher for an assortment of doll hair and began creating various wigs. The class was abuzz with excitement at what I might be up to. I was going to do this and I was going to do this right!

✝

The day finally came and my wigs were complete. Time slowed as the teacher introduced my scene to the class. My confidence was through the roof and I knew my skit would be a complete success.

✝

I threw on a wig, opened my mouth, and the first phrase flew out of my mouth. The class erupted in laughter. To see every single face smiling made me feel so good. I had brought happiness to my entire 4th grade class! I continued and kids were in tears! I punched it into overdrive, completing my mission and earning my title, "The Class Clown." And that was it for me. I was popular and the whole class loved and accepted me. It was one of the best feelings I have ever experienced in my entire childhood life!

✝

My classmates always wanted to be involved in my next skit. Every talent show, my teacher would give me an empty classroom to set up my shows. I experienced a season of being needed and wanted by everyone. It almost seemed like I was a celebrity. I felt like I had a purpose. I knew I was born to cheer those up around me.

✝

Swiftly, the enemy slithered in and stole that away from me though.

✝

Since moving into foster care, I had been dealing with problems with my knee caps popping out of place. They'd constantly pop out,

59

sending excruciating pain throughout my legs. I can remember the pain and the tears very clearly. Nobody really knew what was causing this in me. The doctor's only suggestion was that I needed to exercise my legs more to increase muscle tone surrounding my knees.

One day, we were doing math in our classroom. The teacher was calling us up to the white board one by one to solve the equations. I was a little nervous to be called upon but it wasn't too bad. Right as I was about to be called on, I felt the snap of my knee cap popping out of place. My breath caught in my throat, pain coursing through my legs like electricity. "*Ethan, it's your turn, come on up!*" A few seconds went by with all the class's eyes fixed on me. "*I can't*", I said, trying to hold back tears. "*Why can't you? It's your turn, come on up here.*" "*I can't!*" I uttered as tears began to spill down my cheeks. "*My knee is popped out of place!*" I lost it. I mean completely lost it. I couldn't hold it back. The pain took over me and I began to sob like a baby in front of all my classmates. My social

status in my classroom took a change for the
worse after this ordeal.

Later that year, my class was on our way to visit
Michigan's capital. It would be the longest trip
that I had ever been on alone without my parents
next to me. The plan was for the class to stay in
Lansing for two nights while touring various
important places.

The first sign of change in my status was when
we loaded the bus and nobody would let me sit
with them. I didn't understand and it stung
deeply. I shrugged it off as nothing at first. The
night seemed to be improving. We stopped for
dinner at a buffet and I was in paradise as I
gobbled down the things I never got at home.
After this, we excitedly returned to the bus.
When we got to the hotel, nobody wanted to

share a room with me so I had to room with a teacher and another boy in my class that they labeled a "less than desirable." (He would later go on in life to commit suicide.) Rejection infiltrated my mind and marched through my being like the Nazi regime. I started to lose confidence in who I thought I was. I couldn't understand how my success could falter so quickly. Again, I shrugged it off as nothing. The final crushing blow would come the next day.

   We visited the capital building, a museum, and the Spartan Stadium. College students walked us through the facility and later we were released to run free on the actual turf of the famous Spartan football field. (For such a moment of immense freedom, I didn't feel too free!) Lunch time finally came and the college had a buffet style lunch set up for us. I loaded up my tray and was seated with everyone but forgot something so I got back up. When I returned, my tray had been moved to the far end of the table, away from everyone else and back into the territory of the "less than desirables." I couldn't even eat my

lunch I was so sick from the feeling of rejection.
(Now, thinking back on the situation, I believe
showing my weakness in class when my knee
caps popped was the cause of this domino
effect.)

    I have brushed these memories off until the
Lord recently brought them back to my mind.
I've been praying that He'd show me areas where
rejection came into my life. I never really thought
about it until now. Everything is starting to make
perfect sense! God is connecting the dots and
showing me the hidden plans of my enemy.

    I've found that He'll often do that. Here I am
writing a book about rejection and He's healing
me of all my past rejections! I'm being healed,
with you, throughout this book! How cool is
that? Our God is so majestic! Every day, we can

choose to move one step closer to God, or two steps back. It's kind of like wading into water. First, you get your feet wet. As you adjust to the changing temperature, you slowly move forward, the water now up to your knees. As time progresses, you move to waist deep, then shoulders, then finally, you're in past your head, fully submerged in the love of our Creator. I've gotten "cold feet" before and gotten out of the water on numerous occasions. I'm willing to admit that. It's not something I'm particularly proud of. I know that my honesty will help others though. I'm willing to be an example so that others might not have to go through the same things that I have. I'm telling you, with every fiber in my being, give it all to God! There is no other way! You can search your whole life here on earth and you'll never find anything better than Him! Go ahead, dive in!

I will never leave you; I will never abandon you.

HEBREWS 13:5

FOUR EYES

THOUGH SAD, THIS STEREOTYPE IS
INDEED USED BY BULLIES.

A kid with glasses becomes an instant target of
bullying. I would always wear my brother's
glasses. I thought it was so fascinating to be able
to see things so far away. Who knows? Maybe I
really did need them. Come to think of it, during
assignments in elementary school, it was
extremely difficult for me to see the board. It was
a difficult decision for me when I finally decided
to get them. Half the household already had
them, but I knew what went along with wearing
glasses. Plus, the fact that I was transferring to a
new school didn't help one bit.

For two years, I'd been under the teaching of
my favorite teacher, Mrs. Bower. Instead of

getting a new teacher after 4th grade, the whole class had her again for 5th grade. This made leaving for a whole new school in 6th grade even more devastating! I remember getting anxiety attacks during my whole summer vacation. I couldn't enjoy one day as thoughts overwhelmed my mind. I imagined my future misfortunes of not fitting in. Especially with my new glasses. In my mind, I was already an outcast.

My old school had been freshly built so moving into an older building didn't cushion the move one bit. Everything was old. The school had an odd smell when you walked through the doors. It was an old, musty smell that reminded me of an antique shop. Everything felt awkward and off about this place. Instantly, I became a target.

One morning, I was eating my french toast when a group of kids at my table started pointing at me. "*Look at four eyes! It looks like he even has a unibrow! I bet he shaves it!*" I inhaled my food and went to the restroom to be alone.

A bigger kid in my class immediately took a liking to teasing me. He endlessly assaulted me. If I was holding books, "*BAM!*" onto the floor they went. Wherever I went, there he was right behind me. His goal, to embarrass me as bad as he could. Whenever I said anything, he would mimic and mock me. He would get right into my personal space just to intimidate me. It annoyed me immensely. I grew to hate 6th grade. Not only was I being bullied by this kid in my class, but I'd always encounter others throughout the school that wanted to pitch in as well.

I was trying to get my school work done one day and another one of the bully's victims came over and stabbed me in the hand with a sharpened pencil! I couldn't believe it or understand the purpose behind it! (Now I believe he was trying to show off in front of the bully to make him think that he was tough.) The kid was sent to the principal's office as I went to wash and bandage my fresh wound.

In gym class, we all sat huddled on the cold hard floor around the gym teacher. My daydreams would begin. I fantasized about climbing the walls and swinging from the rafters like a super hero. In my mind, I could see my whole class gazing up at me in complete and utter amazement as I ran around the walls. I was finally accepted. But then I'd be snapped back to reality by the shrill screech of the teacher's whistle.

It amazes me to think back on what I've been through and who I am now. So much negativity followed me around my whole childhood. Rejection should have been my middle name! But the Lord is faithful! Not only did I survive but now I share an intimate, personal background with numerous other people. I'm not ashamed of my past. I'm bringing it all to the light! What is there to be ashamed of? That the devil put a target on my heart and my soul? That only confirms God's great plans for me! The same is true for you! The enemy doesn't want us to succeed. He wants us to fold and give in, to take earthly remedies for our pain and trauma. Those "remedies" never last though. The Bible tells us that a righteous person is someone who gets knocked down, but instead of staying down and regressing towards the world's standards, gets back up. He brushes himself off and keeps pursuing God and His holiness. If you get caught up, get up and keep marching forward! Even Jesus was bullied. He didn't let it get Him down. Instead, He prayed for His accusers. We can overcome someone who hurts us through prayer, forgiveness, and the love of our Lord, Jesus Christ!

You Lord, give perfect peace to those who keep their purpose firm and put their trust In you.

ISAIAH 26:3

YOU'RE A MUTE!

THERE IS LIFE AND DEATH IN THE
TONGUE.

With not much self-esteem, I tried to make it
until my next year of middle school. I got
spooked like a deer in the woods and my face
had been the canvas for every shade of red in the
color spectrum. I've been witness to many
different clichés and sometimes I actually caught
myself longing to be a part of them. I knew my
other classmates felt different about me so I'd try
to keep to myself and not talk to anyone. I guess
I learned to get comfortable with being an outcast
because I didn't mind the school day. To me, it
was better than being at home, which was hell for
me. My school day consisted of intense study
and focus that shut all outside noise out. It was
almost as if I was in my own little world. Come to
think of it, I remember early on coming up with
a peculiar daydream. In it, the "real" me could
transport out of my body and into a safe
comfortable room, while my physical body was
actually a robot completing my daily tasks.

Thinking about it now makes me sad. At such a young age I was so desperate to escape and seclude myself from the world. I knew I was a loner and I enjoyed it.

That's what the enemy wanted though. That's what he desires for everybody. God created humanity to need each other. Being a Christian is all about working together and being built up by others. It's so easy for me to slip back into my old way of life but I know this isn't God's will for me. He made both you and me to speak out His glory. We are vocal creatures with power! We can speak life or death to people and words really do hurt. We need each other. We really do!

One day, it was gym class. I didn't enjoy it too much because of the uncomfortable stretching

72

routines and the overwhelming odds that I might do something wrong and be made fun of. Also, what made it even worse is that I had a major crush on one of the girls in this class. (It just so happened to be a teacher's daughter!) All the guys liked her and she was always the talk in the locker room. I was minding my own business that day and suddenly a deafening voice shouts out, "He's a mute! He's a mute!" I look around to see what's going on and realize that I'm the target of this random phrase. A boy who was known for his mental disabilities was pointing his finger at me and repeating the line over and over again. In my shame and embarrassment, I didn't utter one peep. I wished I could just vanish. The whole gym class had their eyes locked on me and there was nothing I could do but look down at my sneakers. I felt so humiliated as those words were hammered into my fragile mind. I actually began to agree with him. "*I hardly talked to anyone so this must be my identity. I'm a mute.*", I thought to myself.

I forgot about this whole incident until just recently, it went running through my mind. I believe the Lord brought it to the forefront because it is something that needs to be dealt with. Looking back, what happened seems so out of the blue and demonic. It was almost like the enemy used that boy as a vessel to speak to me and bring me tighter into his grasp. My whole life, especially after that day, I've had a hard time opening up to others and being vocal in public. Unrealistic scenes always flash through my mind to hold me back. This puts me right in the devil's court. I feel such a calling on my life to be an evangelist and to preach the gospel to the lost and dying. But if I'm too afraid to speak, how can I walk out my God given destiny? Maybe you've had a similar experience. Maybe the Lord is speaking to your heart right now. Nothing is impossible for our God! His call on your life is stronger than the devil's and by His blood and what He did on the cross for us, you can overcome and be victorious in all circumstances!

People were overwhelmed with amazement. "He has done everything well," they said. "He even makes the deaf hear and the mute speak."

MARK 7:37

ZOMBIE NERD

WHO EVER SAID ZOMBIES COULDN'T BE SMART?

When I was first adopted, I noticed something strange with the other children. Every morning mounds of pills would stretch the countertop. Every kid would grab their "pile" and have to sit criss cross applesauce on the living room floor for a half an hour before their meds kicked in. Almost immediately I was put on medication as well. I was put on a drug called Adderall. My adopted parents informed me that I had ADHD. I was too hyper. Now looking back, I know that all kids are hyper. It's in their DNA. They started me off slow, 5 mg each morning. I would be allowed to get up before everyone else, take my pill and read books in the living room. I remember each doctor's visit they would add 5 mg until I was finally "zombified" at a steady 30 mg. They made sure that I knew that they were in control. A love/hate relationship began with my new medication. The positives were as follows: I had a sharp sense of focus earning straight A's, they gave me a steady buzz, and everything around me suddenly became more interesting. The negatives were: shyness, and extreme anxiety. Nervousness would overtake me and make me shake with fear just from waiting at the bus stop. Unrealistic scenarios constantly played out in my head. I couldn't retain a friendship with hardly a fly because I was so shy. I kept to myself taking on the complete persona of a classified, "nerd." My grades were great, usually straight A's. But what I would have given to have stepped out of my comfort zone and be released from my mental prison! In my eyes, it wasn't fair! I never chose this lifestyle. It was forced on me!

Every day was a struggle. I was the literal definition of shy. Eventually I caught on to the cause of my paranoia, realizing that my pills were making my life a living hell. As mentioned in my other book, *Lost and Found*, I soon quit taking them, and hid them in my safe. (Somehow, I didn't realize that this would be the first place my adopted parents would look if I was trying to hide something!) They found the pills while I was at school. I returned and was accused of drug pushing. It took me by surprise. As a result, everything I ever owned was stuffed into trash bags and taken out with the trash. The trash man came the next day. Anguish and horror filled me as my childhood disappeared before my eyes. The things that I held dear to my heart were just thrown away and I believed, in that moment, that I should have been thrown away too. I believed the lie that I was worth nothing. So many things kept happening in my life that just reinforced that idea.

My few weeks without anything was torture. It was humiliating. All my other siblings had valuables except for me. I felt like an outcast. I was downtrodden and miserable not knowing my worth in the eyes of my Savior.

If only I had known the truth! I believe He was with me though, because I made it through to where I am now. Even though my heart wasn't purely dedicated to Him, He still loved me the same.

Years went past with that lie of worthlessness branded to the forefront of my mind.

Still searching as an adult for something to fill my void, I made an appointment with the doctor and he put me back on the pills. I craved them for all the years I had been off them but here I was again, feeling the same sensations I had as a kid. It wasn't long before I started abusing them. Hanging out with the wrong crowd, I learned how to take the capsules apart, crush the beads inside, then snort them like a line of cocaine. It felt so good! I remember being so focused and energized that I couldn't even sleep at night. I would pop in a video game and wouldn't go to bed until I beat the whole thing! Even after staying up until 8 in the morning it was still hard for me to fall asleep. The rush they gave me made me feel invincible! I felt like I could do anything! But then I'd try, and I'd be so self-conscious in public that I'd be completely miserable.

I was searching for something to give me hope. Before I was 21, I had searched the whole world 100 times over! Nothing satisfied! Nothing does or can but the One who created you! I don't care who you are, I know you can relate to me. Trying that next relationship because you think if you could just get the right one, your life would be perfect. Or maybe if you could find the perfect balance of getting high, grabbing that white rabbit and snuggling close for eternity. It doesn't work that way! You were made to get high, but on the love of your Creator! All that other "stuff" is just counterfeit! It's fake, manufactured by the arch enemy of God, Satan himself! Or maybe you're stuck on porn, and the lust consumes you. You might be so far gone that it feels like you can't control it. That lust you're having with those other women is supposed to directed to the life mate that God has made just for you! See the devil will try anything to get you away from God. Like I said before, he's been studying us for thousands of years! Our enemy knows our weaknesses, but take heart because the cross of Jesus Christ trumps any evil desire or urge satan might toss your way. The blood of Jesus and His sacrifice is stronger! God is stronger! What you're seeing is just a mirage! You're eating crumbs and following scraps that lead you to Hell when God wants to give you the feast that leads to His Kingdom! I'm heading in that direction. The question is, will you come with me?

You, God, are my God, earnestly I seek you; I thirst for you, my whole being longs for you, in a dry and parched land where there is no water.

PSALM 63:1

SOUTHERN HOSPITALITY

IN MY EXPERIENCE, PEOPLE ARE
FRIENDLIER IN THE SOUTH.

But no matter where you go, you can never
escape someone with cruel intentions towards
you. You'll find them a dime a dozen no matter
what part of the country you're in! I found that
out the hard way!

It started out as a family move to Tennessee. I
remember we'd always go down for spring break.
My adopted parents had a double wide down
there that they were renting to a relative. It was
always fun to see the hills turn to mountains and
the black highways turn to red. It would usually
take about a day to reach our destination and by
the time we arrived, we were more than ready for
the chance to stretch our legs.

Things were a lot different down south than
one would expect up north. Hospitality was the
"norm", which I wasn't used to. I mean, most
people have a generic good attitude about
themselves, but in the south, they go out of their
way to show it!

Every direction one happens to glance in
Tennessee is a country setting. This is something
that took a little while to get used to. We were
allowed to ride our bikes to the stop sign, a trip
that took us through the winding roads, past
black walnut trees, and down an extremely steep
hill. On one of our trips, I remember a school
bus drove by and all the kids put down their
windows and started yelling profanities at us.
This shocked me and was my first encounter
with hostility instead of hospitality in the south.

Eventually, we took the plunge and instead of just coming down here every spring break, we opted to call it our home. I wasn't too thrilled about the idea of packing up once again and starting all over, but I knew that there was nothing I could do about it.

The first time we walked into the school for enrollment didn't help. It was almost as if we took a time machine back to the 1950's. I don't know why it felt this way to me but it just did. All the girls were in dresses with bows in their hair and the whole atmosphere just reflected a past time. Quite honestly, it was a little freaky at first. The whole ordeal took me way out of my comfort zone and I felt that I would never fit in.

My first day, I was very shy, and quite frankly, I didn't care. I really didn't want anyone to bother me. Once and a while girls would surround me and ask me to say something because of my northern accent. I would, and they would retreat in hysterical giggling. I didn't mind this too much. In a way, it made me feel like I was kind of accepted.

I got through most of my classes okay. They weren't particularly amazing classes but they were all way better in comparison to my history class. When I reached this class, I awkwardly found an empty seat next to a cheerleader. She tried to make small talk with me. (Like I said before, it was awkward.) Then to make matters even worse, the history teacher decided to call me up to the front of the class to introduce myself. It was my worst nightmare! He wasn't really nice about it either. He was a pretty stern guy.

He'd always give pop quizzes too. And if one of us got a bad grade, the whole class suffered. I think I was even yelled at for not calling the teacher sir! I was miserable! I was so happy when that school year ended and I was able to start a new year in the high school.

I ended up getting pretty comfortable. I barely had any friends but that was okay with me. I just wanted to keep to myself and drift by. But my decision cost me. I was always the brunt of every joke and made fun of by many. Each day I was stomped lower and lower into the mud. I was the jock's guinea pig. Wherever I went, they ended up finding me. There was no escape so I accepted it.

To cope, I started going to a church up the hill
from our house. It was a little southern church
with all the charm a southern church could offer.
At first, I was a little out of place because things
were so much different. But eventually I learned
to love it. One of the worship singers took
interest in me and my siblings and began to
personally teach us. She and her husband would
take us to their house to watch Christian movies
and eat snacks. But our adopted parents soon
began to say that there must be an ulterior motive
about them and forbid us from spending time
with them any longer. Not only that, but I began
to be made fun of for reading my Bible and
mocked openly, mostly by my adopted father. I
began to feel really alone.

Even though my heart didn't completely belong
to the Lord yet, I stilled prayed every day. I
remember being depressed and praying while

hanging clothes out on the clothes line. I looked up and saw a rainbow completely encircling the sun and was brought comfort by thinking of God's promises.

One day, we woke up, and our parents had the weather turned on. They were speaking of stormy weather but I shrugged it off and went to school. All day long, students were talking of possible tornados. When we got home, the sky was olive green and the clouds were swirling like crazy. I believe the tornado sirens started going off. All of us rushed to the basement. I made sure to grab my Bible. My siblings were scared and so was I. I began to speak positively over the situation and told them that God would protect us. Within twenty minutes, all threats were gone of a touchdown and we ran outside rejoicing.

At times, we feel alone, forgotten even. Sometimes we're completely rejected and written off as outcasts. Sometimes we're put into scary, uncomfortable situations. But know this, no matter what, God is with you through every lonely night, every uncomfortable situation, and every storm. There's no strings attached with God! He made you and is madly in love with you! He is waiting patiently for the day when you'll give your whole heart to Him the way He gave His to you!

My grace is sufficient for you, my power is made perfect in weakness.

2 CORINTHIANS 12:9

FIFTH O' JACK

Approximately 187,000 people die from overdoses each year.

I was almost one of those statistics. It started with some stuff at school. An incident happened in which my ex created a rumor that I had a gun and a hit list. (You can also read this story in my other book, *Lost and Found*.) As you can imagine, this would send anyone trembling into their inner shell for security. Psychologists say humans will make one of two choices when a problem arises: fight or flight. I chose flight. United Airlines to be exact! After reaching the pinnacle of popularity in my high school career, this false accusation was a devastating blow to my self-esteem. Let's back track a little.

When I finally reached the age of 16, my adopted family contacted my biological mother in order that we might rekindle our relationship. Even though it was against standard protocol, they allowed me to spend the summer with my mother. It was a very exciting time in my life! Everything seemed so fresh! I felt so free! I was finally unsupervised to do what I wanted all...summer...long! It was great and amazing and spectacular, all wrapped neatly in a little package! I couldn't believe my luck! Like I said earlier, I was a hopeless romantic at heart. My summer was going fine. Now all I needed was a girl to call my own. I didn't know anyone in town so I got kind of desperate. (You know you're desperate when you ask your mother if she knows any single girls!) Surprisingly, she did know a single girl! In fact, she even had her picture on hand! Looking back on the situation, my brother showcasing his girlfriend everywhere he went didn't help me. I probably would have been content playing video games all summer. But then my hormones kicked in. The connection was made and soon I was strolling the town, holding a stranger's hand, not knowing the storm that was brewing in my near future. The weather guys are right! Be prepared for anything! Have a plan! I sure in the heck didn't! Anyways, a weird relationship was formed. I didn't care though

because I finally had a girlfriend. The summer
was an emotional rollercoaster. I cried a lot, even
to the point of hyperventilating and having a
major breakdown. And I mean major! Let's not
get into that right now. My new girlfriend and I
had a pretty strong bond with another couple.
Even though there was not much to do, we'd find
stuff to do. One of our favorite activities was
strolling next to the lake and talking to one
another. This time in my life was a dream come
true compared to my past as the "zombie nerd"
that nobody wanted to talk to. This was a
complete breakthrough for me! I was off my
meds and out of my shell for one of the first
times in my life! The rush was exhilarating! I'd
compare it to skydiving! I was free to let go and
not care what others thought.

One night my girlfriend and her friend came
up with a plan. It was a plan of revenge against
our high school. Their whole lives they wanted to
be popular but instead they were considered
"outcasts." (What can I say? We had a lot in
common!) Their plan was for me, as the new kid,

91

to become popular and then humiliate those that were also popular by a public display of humiliation. I told them, "*piece of cake!*" From that day on a confidence grew in my heart that I believed in. Finally, I believed that I could in fact be popular. I just needed a shot at a place where no one knew me! I put my trust in my own confidence and thought my new-found confidence would never let me down. After all, it was all to impress my sweetheart so I knew I could do it! I took off and I took off fast! I talked with everyone, blurring the lines of everyone's social status. I surprised even myself! I just let go and it was paying off! My social ranks began to soar and I grew more and more popular by the day! Our plan was working, except for one little thing. I wasn't going to go through with the last part of the plan, the humiliation and unfriending. They began to stew in bitterness and resentment as I left them behind in the dust. I should have known beforehand, but I didn't. They came up with a new plan to humiliate me instead. They started a rumor that I had a gun and a hit list. I was arrested in front of the whole school and I immediately let go of my confidence. I said in my heart that I would never let myself get hurt again, an oath that the devil uses against to this day! I'm still struggling to get free from it! But I know my God will deliver me!

After the rumor, I was so humiliated that I dropped out of school. My brother who was a chief of nuclear medicine at the time, came and took guardianship of me and moved me out to Boston. While living there, I began to miss my hometown and against my brother's wishes, I moved back. Instead of facing my fears and going back to regular high school, I opted to go to an alternative school where my other brother was going. Deep down it saddened me because at this new school, I never learned anything. It was a free for all! Students were coming to class high and drunk. It was like one big party. One big party that I was never invited to!

One day, I was talking with my brother before we boarded our bus. Suddenly, from behind us a gruff voice yelled, " *What did you just say about me?*" I turned around to see a rough looking

teen with blonde scraggly hair and blue eyes.
Even though I never said anything about him, he
put me on his radar immediately. And just to top
it off, he was riding the same bus as me. A
nightmare unfolded that day on the bus. A group
of kids joined in with him and taunted me. I
started getting punched in the back of the head
repeatedly. I looked up to see the bus driver was
watching but she didn't do anything. Somehow,
one of the kids learned about my past. "*You
think you're so tough bringing a gun to school?*",
he sneered. I heard in the background, "*Your
brother's an idiot, isn't he?*" I hear my brother's
voice, "*Yeah he is!*" Shameful, humiliating rage
boiled inside me. I felt as if everyone on the bus
was trying to tear the flesh from my bones. Time
slowed and fear crippled me. I froze in my seat
as kids poked and prodded me. I felt like I was
in Hell being tormented by actual demons.

When we finally got to my bus stop, I rushed
off the bus and stormed into my mom's house
with tears streaming down my face. I yelled and
just lost it. I can't believe that my own brother

turned against me! My mom wouldn't say
anything about the situation. That just made me
feel even worse. Hate began to seep through my
pores like worms going deeper and deeper.

That night, I convinced an older relative to
come over and watch scary movies with us. I
thought she was the most fun out of my whole
family. She had short pink hair and was really
hyper. That evening, she provided me comfort
by giving me tips on how to make people leave
me alone by acting crazy. The next school day, I
shoved big safety pins through each of my ears
and coated my eyes in thick mascara.

I began to go down a dark trail of depression. I
knew of only one thing at the time that would
drown it out. Alcohol.

My mom ended up taking a trip to visit my brother in Boston so my brother and I had free reign of the house. Immediately I called our relative again and told her to pack some stuff and come stay with us to keep us company. Bad choice on my part. We watched a bunch of movies but I craved something more. I know she'd buy alcohol for me. I asked her and she agreed to buy me a fifth of Jack Daniels.

My good friend introduced me to a church about a mile from my house. There were lots of other teens and I just wanted to fit in. I wanted to be the cool kid. I ended up going to youth service completely wasted. One of the leaders noticed me and took me into a room with other adults. "*Are you drunk?*" they asked me. I admit to it. They agree not to get the police involved and let me off with a warning. I look up to them and decide not to come to church trashed

96

anymore. This was not for the sake of God (I didn't accept Him yet). I agreed only because I didn't want to get in trouble!

   Later, I went with my relative on a drug run and we ended up getting some methadone wafers. When we got back to my mom's, my relative took a few. I watched and decided that I didn't care anymore. I wanted to get high too. "Can I have some?" I asked. Surprisingly, she handed me some. I felt accepted and downed it. We settled in to watch more movies. I wasn't feeling much of an effect so I asked her for another one. I swallowed it down with a swig of Jack. Next thing I remember, I was hyperventilating. My heart felt like it was going 1,000 miles per hour and I had the cold sweats. I woke up a day and a half later. Nobody even bothered to call an ambulance!

Every one of us has a void within. It's a void that we try to fill with absolutely anything! We run to anything that will help us forget and lose touch with reality. For some it's food, or shopping, video games, or porn, etc. God is the ultimate healer and He can fill that void. But only if we allow Him to! He won't force Himself on us! That wouldn't be free will! That's why we always have that nagging feeling that something just isn't right. That's why that "something" you choose to fill the void never fully satisfies you. A high only lasts so long! You may drink to lose touch with reality but it doesn't last. God wants to be that high you are chasing! We were created to get high, just not on earthly things. That's why we have those cravings! I've been high on numerous occasions but they pale in comparison to the highs I've had on God's presence! He is our drug!

Do not get drunk on wine, which leads to debauchery. Instead, be filled with the Spirit.

EPHESIANS 5:18

BASH BROTHER

ONE OF THE HARDEST REJECTIONS TO
BEAR IS BEING REJECTED BY A BEST
FRIEND.

I had a hard time finding friends. Rejection has
followed me like the plague my whole life. The
devil knows how to throw salt on our wounds.
He's an expert on mankind.

   I was at work one day, and my former best
friend came in to buy something. I say "former"
because he has rejected me as his close friend. I
believe he did this because of my new-found faith
in God. I greeted him on the way out and he
basically ignored me. He acted as if I was just a
piece of scum. It stung. A lot! It kind of took me
off guard and surprised me. We used to be so
close. Even though we were into the wrong things

and not following the Lord, when we were bored, we had fun! I will just put it that way!

We became friends almost immediately when I started going to my hometown high school again. Right when things started turning with me and my ex, this friend and I clicked.

At one point in time, I was living in my ex-girlfriend's best friend's house. It was an awkward situation and living environment for both myself and them. Soon my ex started bringing another guy around and they'd sit on the couch and make out right in front of me. (I swear it was just to get to me!) After all, I still had feelings for her. Soon it was so much that I exploded in anger. I packed my stuff and moved in with my biological mom.

The next day, I was in the high school hall, casually hanging with my so-called friends. That's' when my ex walked in and announced *"He's not supposed to be around us, our parents said!"* She exclaimed enthusiastically to the whole group. A circle soon formed around me. A kid two times my size said, *"Let's bounce him!"* He got right into my personal space. That's when I met my new best friend. He slammed the guy right into a locker and everyone split up. We found out that we had history class together. Our friendship grew substantially within the first few days and soon I was hanging out at his house often. It was a couple blocks away from my mom's. We started smoking and drinking, doing anything to get a buzz. We talked about everything. I had never been so close to anyone. (If your familiar with the Old Testament, our friendship was almost like David and Jonathan's relationship. Almost, but without God!)

For years, our relationship flourished, that is until the one incident where everything slid downhill.

My pregnant girlfriend, (now wife), and I were staying with my mom for a while because we didn't have money saved up to get our own place. My mom started bickering about something and before we knew it my girlfriend's mom was dragged into the conversation. My girlfriend was usually pretty calm mannered until that point. My mom told her to get out and that was pretty much that. My girlfriend gathered a few things and then she was gone. All this put me over the edge so I called up my best friend and asked if I could stay with him for a while. He agreed and met me at my mom's. A lot of verbal fighting occurred and my friend took my side and backed me up against my mother's rants. It was teeth gritting as we began packing all my stuff. I just wanted to be out of that atmosphere. My girlfriend and I had been accepted into an apartment complex but we still couldn't get in for a week yet. I stored most of my stuff in my buddy's garage and put my necessities in his bedroom.

☦

As all this was going on, I was attending college to get my CENA (Competency Evaluated Nursing Assistant) certification. I'd never really wanted to do this as a living. It just seemed like the easiest and fastest course to success for me. The night came for my college refund to come in. I had taken out a little extra money and that night my refund came on a card, about $3,700 to be exact. My friend and I went to the ATM and I withdrew it all. It was the most cash I had ever held in my hands at one time. My buddy was driving and I put the money on his dashboard. We ran a few errands and then I noticed the money was missing. I didn't immediately assume that he would steal from me because we were so close. I gave him the benefit of the doubt. It quickly became apparent that he was guilty. It took about an hour of convincing to get it back. After explaining how much trouble my girlfriend and I would be in without the money, he reluctantly went back outside and then returned, money in hand. This was when I first realized that our relationship was slipping and I knew I couldn't trust him anymore.

My girlfriend and I finally got our apartment and I moved out of my friend's house. We started hanging with the wrong crowd and soon our apartment was broken into. All of our stuff was either stolen or destroyed. My "friend" told me he knew who did it. We moved in with my girlfriend's parent's out of fear.

One night my friend and his girlfriend came to visit us there. My girlfriend's stepdad flipped out on them and cursed them off the property. After this, we noticed yet another change in my friend. There was nothing I could say to explain to my friend that the outburst wasn't my fault and that I didn't know it would happen. I fell down another

rank as his close friend. I was so angry with her
stepdad for his show of outrage.

Eventually my friend moved out west to pursue
a degree in the automotive industry. We talked
here and there online. He was out there for a few
years and eventually he moved back. I met him
at his house and the atmosphere was sour
towards me. His whole family used to be close
with me but now they all regarded me as trash. I
finally accepted that my friendship was over. It
was a sad day for me. We had come so far
together! It felt as if I really had lost all my
money and more. This friendship meant so
much to me! Rejection sucker punched me
square in the gut and the devil had his way with
me.

It wasn't until later when I was working with a friend from church at a factory that I learned the truth behind my prior friendship faltering. It turns out his mom used to work at the same factory. She tried everything to get my new Christian friend fired before getting caught in the act. It's then that I realized, it wasn't a physical thing, but a spiritual thing. I lost my friendship the moment I gave my life to the Lord.

Jesus went through every trial known to man. Sometimes you may feel like you're the only one, but always remember that He has been through it all and overcame it all! So, when a best friend turns their back on you, just remember how Judas Iscariot backstabbed Jesus. He knows the pain of rejection, especially from friends.

When you're a child of God, rejection loses its power. All of it! Who cares if the whole world rejects you and treats you like an outcast! The One that created you accepts you and that's all that matters! You're not an outcast. You've been hand-picked out of this world. You are chosen and set apart. The only reason the world rejects you is because you don't belong to the world. You belong to God!

Coming to Him, a living stone rejected by men but chosen and valuable to God, you yourselves, as living stones, are being built into a spiritual house for a holy priesthood to offer spiritual sacrifices acceptable to God through Jesus Christ.

1 PETER 2:4–5

BLACK SHEEP

I WAS COMPLETELY NAÏVE ABOUT HOW PEOPLE WOULD VIEW ME AFTER MY TRANSFORMATION.

When I completely gave my heart to the Lord, I never realized the backlash that I'd receive from my biological family. Here I was, nobody had seen me for years and I was pretty much accepted as family. It wasn't the greatest working unit but I was thankful to be able to call a group of people my family.

I was fresh in the Lord, full of His anointing and Spirit, and suddenly I was again spit out and rejected by my entire family. Rumors started flying and mean things were said about me. I'm "intolerant." I'm too "religious." One of the worst things that were said of me is that I was just like my father. Except for just a few, I was completely deleted off of everybody's social media accounts. If I see them in public, I try to be nice and I am just ignored and looked at with disgust.

It is often said that the "Black Sheep" of the family is the disturbed one that needs help. They're often caught up in heaps of drugs and criminal activity. It shouldn't surprise me one bit though because Jesus said that because they persecuted Him, they'll also persecute us. We're not greater than Him. Also, it says in God's word that good will be called evil and evil will be called good. That's certainly how it seems.

It hurts, but it's okay. I know I'm accepted by Jesus and that I am His beloved. And to be completely rejected by family is fine with me. It's all so worth it to really be a true follower of my Lord and Savior. Anything it costs, I'm willing to pay, even my life. That's how much my Lord is worth to me. He is completely priceless! I've counted the cost and He is so worth it! Even the darkest day on earth is filled with joy because I have a hope and a future not based on worldly things! Nothing can shake or take my Lord away from me! Everything else on earth can be taken, but not my Lord! He has given both you and I so much to look forward to! If you've gone through a similar situation where you feel alone and rejected, know that Jesus and I have gone through it too! Know this truth, you are in no way alone or a reject. You and I share the same great Father!

Therefore, since we are surrounded by such a great cloud of witnesses, let us throw off everything that hinders and the sin that so easily entangles. And let us run with perseverance the race marked out for us.

HEBREWS 12:1

PHONE CALL

SOME WON'T LIKE THAT YOU'RE TRYING
TO MAKE A POSITIVE IMPACT.

I found this out the hard way. It was after writing
my first book, *Lost and Found.* I was lined up to
sell my book at my first festival and I was super
stoked. I was feeling pretty darn good! I knew
things were heading in the right direction. So, out
of my blissfulness, I decided to send a signed
copy of my book to one of my favorite authors.

At the time, I was working as the grounds
keeper at a local college. The job wasn't all that
bad. I knew it wasn't what I wanted to do with my
life but it was a stepping stone to get where I
wanted to be, after all, I had to take care of my
family along the way. One of my jobs was to
drive the ATV to each flower bed at the entrance

and water them. I had just filled the water tank and was on my way over when a strange number began calling my phone. I parked the vehicle on the curb and answered not knowing the degradation that was waiting on the other line. "*Is this Ethan Hunt?*", a man asked. "*Yes, this is.*", I replied. "*Hi, I'm with the author you just sent your book to.* (I won't name drop here but the author is nationally known.) *I was just wondering what you thought you were doing?*" "*What do you mean?*", I asked. "*Well, to start off, you sent your book to our office. What in the hell do you think you're doing?*" the man asked, clearly aggravated. "*I just wanted one of my childhood role models to read my book.*" "*How old are you?*" "*I'm 26.*" I replied. "*26! You're way too young to make a difference! You want my advice? Throw your book out. It is no good!*" "*Huh?*" I questioned. I was in shock at what I was hearing from the assistant of one of my childhood heroes. "*You heard me. You can't make a difference. You're too young with no experience. Maybe you could try again in the future, but make sure to leave God out of it. No one wants to hear about your beliefs.*" I stood silent at the other end of the call. I knew it was spiritual warfare going on. It just caught me off guard. "*You're not thinking Ethan!*" "*Hey, this is kind of a bad time, do you care if I call you back at a better time?"* I asked. *"No, you may not!"*

And that was the last time I ever heard from him. I'm not going to lie, for about fifteen minutes, I was extremely discouraged. Rejection tried to sink its teeth into me. It was like I had just gotten off the phone with the devil himself. But soon after, I snapped out of it. I recognized this as the works of the enemy. I don't think he wanted me taking my book to the festival!

The festival was a four day event. I took extra time off from work to make sure I could do it. It was exciting and I knew God's hand was in on it when the manager of the festival let me in for free. I borrowed a table and chairs from a local church and bought a pricey tent. The festival manager told me I could set up early so that I'd be ready the following morning. Two of my good friends pitched in and before we knew it, we had an awesome setup that was sure to draw crowds.

It was late that evening when my wife and I were getting ready for bed. We happened to see the weather and it didn't look good. There were major wind gusts along with heavy rain and lightning forecasted. I couldn't sleep, so I told my wife goodnight and drove down to check on my tent. I stood under it and peace surrounded me. The gentle sound of the raindrops put my mind at ease. I thanked God for the opportunity and drove back home in peace.

The next morning, we packed a cooler and all the essentials for a ten hour day. I excitedly drove to where my tent should have been and was instantly filled with complete and utter horror. All the vendors were set up and hard at work but my beautiful, expensive tent was crumpled up on the ground it was completely demolished. I felt like packing things up and calling it quits right then and there as discouragement swept through my soul. But then I began to realize the strategy of my enemy. I strapped on my spiritual armor that day and went full force, marching straight ahead to victory!

With the help of a close friend, we used duct tape that matched my tent's color and patched the whole thing up. Before we knew it, we were in business and the battered tent became a symbol that mirrored my life. It was beat up but still standing. God spoke this truth to my heart throughout the festival. It became an instant ice-breaker as I described the incident to customers and showed them the before and after pictures. The Lord was really speaking to me.

As we grew more comfortable with our little "business", my eyes and heart were drawn to a couple that reminded me of hippies. They were a cute, young couple, complete with dreadlocks and 70's looking attire. They were in the business of selling rare stones and homemade necklaces. I did a lot of praying for them in my free time. We spoke once and a while and I got the impression that they were into spiritualism similar to buddhism. They talked a lot about positive energy. I knew they were hungry and searching, I wanted so desperately for them to know my beloved Jesus. One day, after business slowed down for a while, I felt led to go across and give them one of my books. The young girl said to me, "You're a Christian, aren't you? I thought about what Jesus must have went through when I got my tattoo on my back." Throughout the festival, we became good friends. They even made me a homemade necklace that really meant the world to me. Jesus loved them through me and I continue to feel that one day they'll know the true power of God. I continued giving my book to the vendors around me but no one drew my attention and heart like the young couple had. They were so curious. I understood why they viewed the world through the lens that

they did. They wanted peace on earth. They just
didn't know the ultimate Peace Giver.

There were so many awesome testimonies that
resulted during the event! One girl came by and
was able to open up about her past trauma. It was
very liberating to be able to encourage others to
tell their past stories in order to help them heal.

As I was busy selling my books, my friend who
was helping me was busy drawing people in. I
couldn't see her for a while but eventually saw
her by the road talking to a lady and using very
animated movements. After about an hour, they
both started walking towards our tent. She had a
beauty about her. Strange scars were scattered
across her face. Come to find out, the lady was
involved in the occult. She had been seeing
demons everywhere! She had a very prominent

scar on her forehead and when we asked her about it she recounted how she believed an alien had implanted her with a device and how she tried to dig it out. She told us out of every vendor at the festival, ours was the only one that radiated light. We evangelized her for what seemed like hours. We prayed with her, pleading with her to rid herself and her household of all her occult paraphernalia. She walked away not fully accepting Jesus as her Lord and Savior but a seed had been planted and we were grateful for the opportunity!

After the lady had left, it was time for the city fireworks at the lake since it was the 4th of July. My confidence in what God was doing through me grew exponentially during those four days. People sat in large crowds for the fireworks but my son took off running on the dock. I quickly got up to chase after him and a lady began to make a scene. She was yelling and swearing at me. I knew it was just the enemy but it was very humiliating and it snapped me back to the reality that I still wasn't fully healed from my fear of man. I sat down with my son and pondered to myself as to whether there would ever come a day when I finally wouldn't care about what others had to say. I needed only to hear His voice.

The next morning was the final day of the event. I felt so refreshed by the whole experience. People constantly came up to me crying and hugging me. Some even said that people at the bar were referring my book to others. I knew in my heart that I was definitely on the right path towards my God given destiny. It felt so good! One older gentleman who was in his 70's came back and bought seven more books to give to his friends and family! He told me that in all his life, he had never taken the time to sit down and finish a book until he sat down and read mine! It amazed me greatly. My initial aim was for the younger generation, yet the Lord was working on the older generation as well!

✝

I had a few more friends stop down to help me on the last day. My books were selling out to the point where I only had a few left! I was so thrilled! As we were chatting, in the distance I saw a news crew walking through and immediately knew in my spirit that they would be drawn to my tent. They approached and asked if they could interview me. I of course agreed. I mentioned a lot about my journey and how others might benefit by starting their own journey. Finally, I shared my faith in Jesus right on camera! It was amazing! Afterwards, the crew mentioned that they were Christians too and that their goal was to get as much air time for Christ as possible! I couldn't believe it! God was working so powerfully on this last day! To top it off, the news crew put down their equipment and we formed a circle and they began to pray with us. They prayed that the Lord would bless us! We said our goodbyes and they were off. I forgot to bless them with a signed copy of my book! I took off after them and ended up being stopped by a couple who saw my shirt which read, "Jesus is my King!" To this they replied, "*He's our King too!*" We had an awesome conversation about how they were planning to produce a website where they would have countless testimonies of other Christians to share with people around the world. They wanted me to be one of their first recordings and made plans to come back and meet with me. We traded information and I blessed them with a copy of my book.

After finally finding the news crew again, I blessed them with one of my books then giddily walked back to my tent where my friends and wife were sitting. I was so excited and absolutely amazed with everything that had just happened! I knew this was part of God's plan for my life. In just four days, I made more money than I did in a month at my day to day job, I knew I could make a living this way and that God would provide for my family!

We packed up and headed to the grocery store on the way home. I had so much confidence as I strolled through the aisles. I felt complete and knew I was on the right path. I was determined to start my plan as soon as possible. My plan was to purchase an RV and travel across the U.S. with my family in tow. I told my wife my plans and she immediately got cold feet and put on the brakes. Not wanting to force her, I agreed to pray about it first and let God speak to me. Boy, did He! And it was not in a way I expected!

We rented the *Teenage Mutant Ninja Turtles* to watch as a family that night. I popped it in and as the movie began it's opening credits, I had a strange urge that God was speaking to me through the words of the narrator. He said, " *You are extraordinary my son! Unlike anything the world has ever seen! Vowed by greatness to protect the people! A dark force is growing... Their leader...who comes at you with veracity, ...will outnumber you. The people will look upon you as their only hope. Eyes focused, elbows locked, stance low. Lead their paths. I*

122

know you are eager to answer their calls but your training is not yet complete. The world below must remain your home. As your Father, you must trust me. Patience, patience. You're not yet ready to go above ground but I believe when that day comes and you rise to the streets, you are going to be responsible for amazing things!"

Chills trickled down my spine as I realized both God's heart and plan for my life. I could feel the Holy Spirit upon me and I submitted to the Lord to wait for His perfect timing.

We all have a purpose. We all have special talents that the Lord has given us. What we do with them is up to us. Will we use them to bring more glory to our Risen Savior or will we hide them in fear? I guarantee you, all the best secular singers that you hear have all been blessed with special talent from the Lord. From Beyoncé to Britney Spears, and from Michael Jackson to Adele. The list goes on and on. God gave them their skills! The question is, are they using their gift for God's glory or for personal gain? We have been put on earth for a purpose. Deep down inside, you know you have a talent or gift. Maybe you've made it public or maybe you're afraid of what people will think. Listen to me though. Tap into that skill and use it all for the glory of the One who gave it to you! What are you waiting for? None of us are guaranteed another day here on earth. Have courage and strength! Not only do I believe you can do it, but the very One who created you is cheering you on as well! You can do it! Nothing can stop you but you when God is on your side!

Live life with a due sense of responsibility, not as those who do not know the meaning of life but as those who do.

EPHESIANS 5:15

PART II THERAPY
SESSIONS

KANSAS CITY

I HAD ALWAYS FEARED THE STORM.
BUT NOW I WASN'T SO AFRAID.

The domino effect happened on my 27th
birthday. My wife, two children, and I were
driving to an indoor waterpark to celebrate.
Suddenly, Kansas City began to flash through my
mind. I told my wife about the urge that
continued to tug at my mind. I mentioned that I
thought God was calling us to move there. We
talked about it and finally agreed that we'd need
a LOT of prayer and confirmation before we
made such a huge commitment.

A few days went by and I felt like I needed to
reach out to the International House of Prayer in
Kansas City. The International House of Prayer
is a ministry whose heart is set on the art of

prayer. They are committed to 24/7 prayer and equipping this generation to be the Lord's army.

I became an admirer of the music that was coming out of this ministry long before I had desire to become a part of their ministry.

Let's go back about five years. My childhood friend was spending a few days at my apartment with me just hanging out. At that time, I was already a believer but he was not. I told him of my experiences with the Lord and he seemed to desire them too. The only problem was, he wanted immediate proof in order to believe. So, I committed to worship with him thinking maybe the Lord would do something supernatural to prove Himself. After hours of worship music, nothing happened to convince my friend that God was real. So, I committed myself to three

days of fasting. Days blurred as my flesh grew
weak and my spirit grew stronger. Soon,
wandering on the internet, I found myself
watching a skit based on a lady named Misty
Edwards. The song was "*People Get Ready.*" It
was so powerful and so dramatic that it pierced
me deep in my heart! Tears flowed as the lyrics
boldly proclaimed the near coming of Jesus. The
lyrics went, "*He's not a baby in a manger
anymore! He's not a broken man on a cross! He
didn't stay in the grave and He's not staying in
Heaven forever! People get ready, Jesus is
coming!*" It inspired me greatly to keep up my
walk with the Lord and to be prepared for His
second coming. That's when I became a fan of
Misty Edward's music. I didn't know then that
she belonged to the International House of
Prayer.

My wife and I kept praying and soon
confirmations came flowing in. As I would have
alone time with the Lord, a certain song would
turn on every single time! The song had to do
with forgiving my father. I felt strongly that my

Healer was yet again healing the deep, dark recesses of my battle-torn soul. Healing and new friendships seemed to be the theme for our move. The fact that the same song came on every single devotion period 14 times in a row confirmed this! I knew this couldn't be a coincidence. Next, we began to have dreams that pertained to our trip and could really feel Godly peace about the whole situation. I woke up one morning and completely lost it, sobbing uncontrollably in front of my wife and children. This was something that had never happened before.

I was at work one night and as my boss left, I turned the radio station to a Christian station. (She had told me that I wasn't allowed to listen to my music in her store because she didn't want to offend anyone.) I was going to listen and obey her instructions but felt very strongly to switch the station. So, I did it. Next, two guys walked in. They walked around looking at everything for a while. Finally, they got to the counter. "*We're Christians too.*", they informed me. We started talking and one of the biggest confirmations happened that still blows me away just thinking about it! The two men were from a Christian camp out in the country. As we excitedly spoke to one another, I shared what the Lord had put on me and my wife's hearts. Suddenly, one of the men excitedly tells me, "*Yeah, my nephew is one of the main worship leaders at IHOP!*" I couldn't believe it! This had to have been a sign from God! What were the chances that two believers would walk into my work, right as we're about to close for the night, and confirm what God had put on our hearts? I was in small town Cadillac, Michigan talking with someone with a big connection to Kansas City! Again, I knew it just couldn't be a coincidence! Joy filled my heart as the two men huddled around me and began to pray that God's will would be done in my life. My co-worker looked on from a distance. My brothers, who I had just met, had just been used as the tools of God Almighty. They made my night! They were off almost as soon as they arrived, but the presence of the Lord still lingered in the air around me and rested deep in my spirit!

Peace and adventure consumed the atmosphere of our house as our minds ran wild with the thoughts of God's plans and purpose for our lives. We were so excited! We couldn't wait to start a new chapter in our lives!

We are still awaiting God's direction on the move. We're not sure if the move to Kansas City is a future event or if it's supposed to happen sometime soon. Please be in prayer for God's clear calling on our lives and future.

Very commonly, in our walk with the Lord, He will put something big on our hearts. After all, we're all made for a purpose. I want to encourage you to surrender to His plans for your life. His dreams for you are so much more than your own dreams are for yourself! He's got great big plans for you but you'll need to surrender your own dreams to Him. He will not lead you down the wrong path! Also, be obedient to what He puts on your heart. Commit to follow his lead no matter how big or small the task might be! You'll be greatly rewarded for your obedience!

Take delight in the Lord, and he will give you the desires of your heart.

PSALM 37:4

THE LIVING WORD

I'VE BEEN PRAYING FOR YEARS THAT GOD WOULD SEND ME A BEST FRIEND.

A friend who loves Him more than I do. I figured that way, he'd constantly be an influence on me to further my relationship with the Lord. I believe He's answered my prayers.

I reached out to a pastor who has been like a father to me during my adolescent years of growing in the Lord. He told me of another pastor, in a different city, whose heart was on IHOP and Kansas City as well. My wife and I decided it would be beneficial to meet with this pastor so we made the 12-mile journey to the church called, "*The Living Word*". It was an interesting place to say the least. From the outside, you could tell by the somewhat rusty roof and pole shed behind the building that it used to be something else. "*They must be very resourceful.*", I thought to myself. We slowly walked in, not knowing what to expect, and were immediately greeted by a woman with joy in her eyes and a warm smile. We felt welcomed and wanted instantly. This was something we had never fully experienced at any other house of God. As we continued to walk, multiple people came and introduced themselves to us. The hospitality was amazing! The church was in the middle of something called Harp and Bowl Worship. It is modeled after IHOP itself and the book of Revelation. Basically, it is the prophetic singing of prayers. Something was much different about this place! We could feel the Spirit of God swirling throughout the air, dancing around us as we breathed Him in. We felt wanted and accepted. My heart started to heal as soon as we walked through those doors!

After service, we talked excitedly with the pastor, telling him what we believed the Lord had laid upon our hearts. He took such genuine interest in what we had to say! We prayed with the pastor and as we were walking out the door, everyone in unison said *"bye!"* with such love! It was as if they had known us our whole lives and we were a close-knit family! We realized something special was happening at this church. We felt an urgency to immediately make it our home church, but we decided to pray about it first.

After praying that night, peace rushed into our hearts like a waterfall. We were sure that we were meant to fellowship with this community of wonderful believers. We just weren't sure for how long. We pondered to ourselves, *"Maybe this is just training before we make our big move."*

As time went on, we realized that this was indeed a special little community. It was a treasure, a gem tucked in the countryside.

Since becoming a believer, I instantly realized that there was something wrong in the "modern church." All I ever heard preached was blessings. (Don't get me wrong, I have nothing against blessings, but this is not the main call of the Gospel!) The messages I heard across varying churches in my new walk were loosely based on the same topics. There were a handful that stood out to preach the full Gospel. This worried and troubled my soul tremendously as I began to feel the burden of the Lord on my heart. When I read my Bible, I read about people who had to battle to get where they were. They didn't just get the "milk and honey". They had to fight for the "Promised Land"! The fights I read about were about practicing selflessness, enduring long-suffering, and developing perseverance. It was never cotton candy, rainbows and unicorns for anyone in the Bible! When Jesus preached, He let us know that we were going to go through

136

some stuff! That's the thing I liked about our new pastor. He wasn't afraid to say it like it was. He just let it flow naturally. (The truth often hurts a lot. But without pure truth, you end up with a lie!) It seemed to me that a lot of people focused on the gifts of God rather than the Gift-giver Himself. It reminds me a lot of what was going on in Jesus' ministry. He had vast multitudes following Him, but once the bread and fish ran out, so did the people. He was left with only a mere few. Jesus said to the crowd, "*Very truly I tell you, you are looking for me, not because you saw the signs I performed but because you ate the loaves and had your fill.*" That's not how I want to live and I want to warn other people not to go that route either because all you'll find is *dry.......dead....... religion*!

As we continued, the pastor and everyone would tease that we were just leaving for a little while to get trained up, then we'd be back. We came in agreement that maybe that really was God's plan for us.

✝

One Sunday, our pastor talked about a fascinating vision that a lady from Detroit had for the little town of Manton in which our church was located. She sent him a message saying that she really needed to get together with him. He was really busy so he put it off until he felt from the Lord that he really needed to meet up with the woman. She went on to tell him of a map that she saw in the vision. Dots filled the map of Michigan and she was confused as to why. Our pastor immediately realized that each dot was over a city in Michigan where a House of Prayer was erected. The lady went on to tell of the Lord stabbing a sword into Manton and drilling until living water erupted. Our church is in the process of building a "House of Prayer" of our very own at the moment! Everything the woman told our pastor began to make sense to me.

I enjoy watching a program called, "*Manna Fest*", hosted by a guy named Perry Stone. Perry has written numerous books and has a really strong gift of prophecy. He actively films his show throughout places in the Holy Land that have been made famous throughout the Bible, lending to the ultimate experience of the show. (I love it!) He started hearing through the Christian community that people were starting to get visions and dreams of something that is about to take place called the "Rural Revival." People will begin to leave the bigger cities in order to take part of the coming revivals that are set to take place in the countryside. Something tremendous is happening in our church's town! Even though it is small right now, it is the fastest growing city in the state of Michigan!

When I first came to the Lord, my heart was so on fire! No amount of water could have put it out! My passion for my God was beyond words, my heart ached for Him. That's how we all should be! All the time! That's what it really means to be a Christian. To be completely and utterly ruined by love! I'm not giving in or giving up. I *will* get back to that point and I hope you'll make it your goal to do the same!

How good and pleasant it is when God's people live together in unity.

PSALM 133:1

REVIVAL WARRIORS

THE PASTOR AND HIS WIFE
FREQUENTLY HELD YOUTH MEETINGS AT
THEIR HOME.

I felt pretty nervous about these meeting because
this meant that we'd be close with other people
socializing. I was scared as unrealistic rejection
scenarios played throughout my mind like a
movie reel. My wife and I prayed that God would
be with us. He sure was that night!

We pulled up to a large house with a bunch of
cars in the drive way. As we walked in, we were
overtaken by the rustic charm of the place. We
could hear many voices and as we walked into
the living room, almost every seat was taken as
the young group lined the whole room. We were
late so we were a little anxious that all eyes would
be on us. Everything went smoothly though as we

found our seats. Everyone was talking
animatedly, and we could just feel the presence
of God in the room, just like we could at the
church. It was as if we had gone back in time,
into the book of Acts where the disciples all
broke bread together and fellowshipped! I broke
out of my comfort zone and began to talk with
everyone. I told them my testimony as well as my
worst fears. I felt so accepted.

As we ate snacks, we began to transition into an
exercise of prophecy. Everyone closed their eyes
and one person would put a penny in someone
else's hand. Our job was to listen to the Lord's
voice on what He wanted to say to that person.
One by one, people began to speak out many
things. In my heart, I was thinking that it would
be amazing if me and my wife got a chance to be
prophesied over! The things that everyone was
saying were hitting so close to my heart. I thought
it was so strange how familiar everything was.
The visions were: joy and a field of flowers with a
sunset, a sun with a banner that said, "Song of
Solomon", flowers blooming, amazing colors,

love, a tree growing and producing fruit, an electric cross, financial blessing, the song "*God's Not Dead*" (let love explode), and a lion.

People took turns prophesying until it was revealed that my wife was the one holding the penny. I was in shock at how accurate the prophesies were!

It turned out to be an amazing night for us. It was late and we didn't want to leave but we had our children with us so we packed up and left. I felt free and relieved at the goodness of my God! He was indeed healing me of my past trauma! I can't say that the devil didn't try to introduce ideas in my mind that I wasn't accepted, but I can say that I fought through and won the lies over with truth!

Just being introduced to this young group of believers set my heart back on fire. I was so encouraged to meet people my age who actually had a strong urge to evangelize to the community. Often, they'd listen for the Lord's voice on who they were to be looking for. They'd write down the various descriptions and once they found that person, they'd show them the list they made, proving that it really was God who led them to that particular person! I know, it's powerful!

†

I want to encourage you. Maybe you've went through such horrible rejection that you feel stuck, and trapped inside a prison. The heaviness seeks to drown you, to crush any attempt that you might make towards obtaining your freedom. You don't have to stay stuck or trapped! There is only one key that can open your cage and His name is Jesus Christ of Nazareth! He's not just

144

some story. He is real, living, and breathing, and He wants to have a meaningful relationship with you! Don't be deceived into thinking that you can protect yourself by never making friends or never getting out. We need each other! The devil wants to separate us from other believers that way we are more vulnerable to his tactics! If we are alone then we are a target, fair game to him! Take that first step. I know you might be scared, but I promise you, God will never leave your side! He is with you. It's time to heal! It's time to start again! Humans were created to fellowship with one another. Without social time with others, we begin to fall into depression. Don't be fearful. I's time to pick yourself up, dust yourself off and try again!

And let us consider how we may spur one another on toward love and good deeds, not giving up meeting together, as some are in the habit of doing, but encouraging one another-and all the more as you see the Day approaching.

HEBREWS 10:24–25

THE GOOD JUDGE

IN ALMOST THIRTY YEARS, I HAD NEVER
ONCE TALKED TO A COUNSELOR.

To be honest, I never thought I really needed
one. It was almost like holding a medal to be
able to boast and say that. Within starting this
book, I've come to the conclusion that I did
indeed need to talk to a counselor. God didn't
make us to be alone or heal alone. Sure, He
could miraculously heal us of our past trauma
within an instant, but sometimes, almost always,
He uses and works through other believers.
These other believers have the impartation of
Jesus Himself within themselves! He quite
literally works through us! Isn't that amazing? It
certainly blows my mind! The puzzle pieces are
all starting to come together for me and I'm
starting to really see God's master plan for all of
humanity! This is just the beginning of my
healing journey and I just know that God will use
me as His instrument to heal others who have
gone through similar circumstances. This is the

beginning and written account of my healing. If
He can do it for me, then He can do it for you!

✝

I decided to open up to our new pastor of the
church we had just started attending. I started
asking him questions, (questions I seemed to
never have answered through anyone else), and
he decided that we needed to set some time
aside each week to talk.

✝

After the rush of first becoming a believer, I've
been dealing with a lot of depression from day to
day. I didn't understand it. I mean, if I'm a
Christian, then why in the world would I be
depressed? I've come to learn that becoming a
believer puts an even bigger target on our backs
for the devil! Now we're not just stagnant rebels,
but we are world changing warriors! And
becoming a warrior means that we're going to

have to fight...A LOT! So that's how I know what a big destiny I have here on earth, from all the unending trials I've been going through. I wake up some days and wonder why I'm even alive. I have no idea why I would think such things, I'm far beyond blessed. A beautiful wife, two beautiful children, a house, a car, food to eat, and clothes to wear. I have no reason to be depressed! I should be one of the happiest people on planet earth because I have Jesus!

The heaviness of this depression is the main reason I opened up to talk to my pastor. I was just sick of holding garbage in, pretending to be a perfect Christian with no problems when in reality, I'm not. Not only was I struggling with depression, but also many insecurities and rejection, as you already know. It was as if a big rock was lodged in my stomach, stopping up anything spiritual that the Lord wanted to do in my life. Finally, I said enough was enough and I scheduled my first appointment for counseling.

The day of my appointment, a snow flurry began, making the roadways very slick to say the least. I'm not going to lie, canceling did cross my mind a few times. It was about a twenty-minute drive from where I lived. I didn't mind. It gave me ample time to free my mind when I wasn't worrying about hitting a patch of ice from time to time. I arrived right on time, nervously parking in the rear of the church. Thoughts fluttered through my mind of possible rejection scenarios. I was scared but had had enough. Whatever the outcome, I was going in!

I made my way to the restroom to stall time. Afterwards, I anxiously knocked on his door. After getting comfortable, I began to relay problems that I had been struggling with for a while. He immediately responded with scripture and knew exactly what I was facing.

It felt good to be understood and listened to. Besides the man who brought me to Christ, no other had ever had the time, let alone the patience, to see me through and just listen to me.

I told him how in my beginning stages of being a Christian, some told me I was too zealous for the Lord. On different occasions, I prayed with different people to take my zealousness away. Now as more of a mature Christian, I realize the dangerous waters I had entered into by allowing this sort of vow. We began to pray for God to stir the fire deep within me once again. I had a vision of a house on fire and began to smell burnt wood. Then my belly and heart felt on fire and a weight was lifted. In turn, I felt power tingling throughout my fingertips.

Next, we moved on to more uncomfortable matters. I opened up about my adopted family always calling me "Chester the Molester." It hurt to dig this deep into my past and be vulnerable to any rejection that he might have over me, but I took a deep breath and told him everything. I related how I was ashamed and humiliated at their false accusations. He invited me to close my eyes and wait for God to speak truth into my situation. I saw "INNOCENT" in red letters and heard and seen a gavel being swung down. Another weight lifted off me as I told him the vision. The cat was out of the bag. I told him how as a teenager, I felt weird and like a creep. We did the exercise again. This time God put special emphasis that I was indeed, "normal." More weight lifted. We prayed and ended the session on positive terms.

On my way home, I thought about our encounter again. I knew for certain that God was indeed healing me of my past, that he had put this man that was after His own heart, into my life for a reason!

Then your face will brighten with innocence. You will be strong and free of fear.

JOB 11:15

FAULTY THINKING

M Y NEXT SESSION WAS SCHEDULED
FOR ANOTHER WEDNESDAY.

I couldn't wait to get on the open freeway and
just let my cares go. I turned on some Christian
rap and I was off. (Christian rap is not as corny as
it used to be, it's actually gotten quite good!) I
pulled in and eagerly walked to my pastor's
office. He was watching IHOP live on the
computer. We got into small talk about how our
church was so similar to IHOP. Afterwards, we
went full fledge into healing mode. We prayed
once again. I mentioned how sometimes it's hard
to get close to God because of my past with my
biological father. (Subconsciously, my mind
seems to not fully trust God. It's a battle I fight
against daily!) He decided that it would be best to
tackle this obstacle that day.

I got still before the Lord and the visions began again. The first were these dark, lanky demonic hands trifling and destroying fresh fruit. The next was trash being thrown out a window. My pastor prayed that God would show me where my mistrust with fatherly figures began. I instantly remembered a time when my walk was fresh with the Lord.

God had put very strongly on my heart to sell my flat screen and *PS3* game system and to give the money to the poor. I sold these prized possessions of mine and heard something in my mind say, "*Did God really want you to give the money to the poor?*" This got me thinking and I decided that maybe I would keep the money and just do what I wanted with it. Long story short, I ended up buying a really expensive pug. (I know, money well invested!) At the time though, I thought it was one of my wisest decisions to date. In reality it was a really a foolish one, especially because we didn't have time for a pet with such high maintenance. I slowly felt myself slipping from my newfound unity with God. One act of disobedience was all it took. I had listened and been deceived by the serpent of old.

✝

I told my pastor about this and he wanted me to get past this hurdle that I thought had brought me low. I explained how I had repented and made it up by donating our pug to a good cause.

✝

One night, we had the news on and a story aired in which a young man had been conned online. He had paid the money for a purebred pug puppy but instead had gotten robbed. It hit me to the core, watching him cry as he told his story. (The weird thing was that I had been praying for a good owner for our pug because we couldn't keep up with his daily needs, we were always so busy!) I knew this was an answered prayer. I called up the news station as fast as I could manage and explained my situation. The news immediately got in touch with the young man and we arranged to meet. The man thanked me repeatedly, eyes fresh with tears throughout our meeting. I had grown attached to our little friend, (We named him, Bowser, I've always been a big Mario fan!) I knew our decision to let him go was the best decision. We said our goodbyes and I gave the man some gospel material and that was that. I felt like I had redeemed my deal with the Lord but the enemy has his ways of holding us in shame. I just didn't recognize it at the time.

I mentioned something about not wanting to get as close to God as possible because I was afraid of getting hurt again, like I had with my real father. Subconsciously, I had linked pleasing my father to pleasing God. I felt like I had to work for His approval. Pastor knew that we needed to get to the "root" of my feelings.

We began again to be still before the Lord. God took me back to when I was a child and to the different places where the enemy had planted lies within me. The first memory was of a day when my brother and I went to work with my father. He cut down trees for a living. This job involved him working a safe distance away from us. This gave us ample opportunity to get into mischief. We decided it'd be fun to throw the décor off the client's porch. When our father was finished with his work, he knocked on the customer's door. Instead of a paycheck, he was met with angry glares. He was told that unless he whooped our butts in front of him, then he would not be getting paid. Our dad needed the money, and even though we probably deserved discipline this time, the humiliation struck deep and left a scar.

The next vision took place at another one of my father's jobs. This job had a dock on a beautiful lake. Our father went to talk with the potential client, we on the other hand decided to explore. At the end of the dock we found a live tank full of fish. We decided they needed to be freed. The owner came running down the dock yelling and swearing. Our father had the job, but lost the job because of us.

I never realized it, but in both instances, I felt like I had lost my father's approval, and this was in turn weighing in on my relationship with God. I started off good with Him. I accepted His Son into my heart, but it was impossible to stay perfect. Everyday life weighed on me and sometimes I made wrong choices. I guess in those wrong choices, I felt like I wasn't good enough to be God's son. It took some genuine therapy to reveal these things to me.

As believers in Christ, we don't have to work for God's approval. We already have it. In scripture, it says our works are like filthy rags before the Lord. (Rags in biblical times would refer to a woman's menstrual cloths. Disgusting, right?) Our works should be something we're led to do, not pushed to do. The Lord leads gently. The devil puts on pressure and pushes. We can never "work our way" to Heaven. It is impossible! That's like saying that Jesus' sacrifice on the cross wasn't good enough! We who believe in God's Son are already legitimate sons and daughters. Our debts have been forgiven!

Because you are his sons, God sent the Spirit of his Son into our hearts, the Spirit who calls out, "Abba, Father." So you are no longer a slave, but God's child; and since you are his child, God has made you also an heir.

GALATIANS 4:6–7

RUBBER CHECK

I WOKE UP AND WAS GOING TO GO
THROUGH MY DAILY ROUTINE, GIVING
THE BEGINNING OF MY MORNING TO
THE LORD.

I was feeling pretty good besides the fact that we
were struggling financially but we were trusting in
the Lord that He'd provide for us.

Long story short, my brother who just got his
license, had some extra money and he wanted to
finally get a working set of wheels. I knew the
perfect place to look because my other older
brother worked at a car lot. We went and looked
at the vehicles that were in my brother's price
range. The first car, the door fell off. The second
would make the tin man jump for joy it leaked so
much oil! My brother decided on the oil leaker. I
told him it was a bad idea. (But what did I know,

I'm just the little brother!) Right when he was
about to sign the paperwork, a customer brought
in a very nice-looking Ford Focus. My older
brother could sell it to my brother at the same
price that he was going to pay for the run-down
vehicle. Everything was looking just fine until we
found out that in order to get the car off the lot,
it'd have to be in someone else's insurance since
my brother was a new driver. His insurance
quote was outrageous and quite frankly, that
should have been a warning sign to me. But, I
pushed the negative thoughts out of my mind
and continued. I decided to give him a chance
putting everything under my own name so he
could get the car off the lot. I fought against my
wife tooth and nail. She was not a happy camper.
I didn't pray or look for guidance from the Lord,
I just did it out of my heart. I took him aside and
informed him that he needed to park the vehicle
in front of my house until we could get it
switched over into his name. I agreed that if he
needed to go anywhere, then I would be in the
car with him and I let him know that he was
NEVER to leave the city. It wasn't that I was
trying to be controlling, I just knew the
consequences if he were to get into a wreck
under our name. A few days after getting the
vehicle for my brother, I called my insurance to
cancel his vehicle on my policy. My plan was to

161

just let it sit until he had the money to switch it into his name. The insurance agent informed me that since I had gotten a license and registration on the vehicle, I would be fined by the state of Michigan for not having insurance on the vehicle. She convinced me to leave things alone. I listened, though I wish I hadn't. My worst nightmare was confirmed a few days later. My father came over and asked if we'd heard about the accident. My heart sank. "*You're joking, right?*", I said hoping it was just nonsense. He informed me that he wasn't, and that my brother had been in a head-on collision with another vehicle. My heart sank even lower. First, I began to feel worried if my brother and the other man was okay or not. Then, anger welled up deep within me. I didn't want to talk about it anymore. I told my father that he should leave and we'll talk another day. As he left, my stress and frustrations erupted like a volcano. My wife started sobbing, "*How could he do something like this to us?*" I tried to council her telling her that even if we lost everything in this world it wouldn't matter because we would still have Jesus. The next day, I called up my insurance agent again. She told me that since my brother was not on the policy and wasn't supposed to be driving the vehicle in the first place, that my wife and I would be held responsible for all damages, all hospital bills, and that our insurance would probably sky rocket in price. I was so frustrated! Nobody informed me that the vehicle had been in a crash! Not my brother! Not the police! Nobody! I didn't know what to do. I was between a rock and a hard place. My other brother and I went from place to place the next day, retracing the broken mess my other brother had left for us. We started at the impound yard and found the once beautiful little sports car now completely demolished. We opened the door and immediately found alcohol. Disappointment was all that I could feel. I had a man to man conversation with my brother and really thought I could trust him. I really did. The impound yard directed us to their office. Once there, I tried to explain the situation to the man that was in charge but was met with a nasty attitude. We tried talking to him but he cut us off mid-sentence, "*It's not my problem, it's yours!*" He then switched the bill from my brother's name to my name. "*Great!*", I thought to myself. "*Just what I needed, more debt.*" I forgave the man and moved on. Afterwards, I played phone tag with two police stations that were involved with the crash. (I still don't have a police report or any solid evidence of what had happened that night.) After talking with one of the policemen in person, I found out that I could either prosecute

163

my brother for a potential 10-year felony, or let the whole thing go. We decided that we couldn't do that to him. We let him go.

I was standing under the warm water of the shower when I heard a voice like many waters say, "*ETHAN! DO NOT BE AFRAID!*" It was such a calming and peace filled voice! It brought joy to my heart instantly and my worries ebbed as I realized that it was the voice of Jesus Himself. Then as I was brushing my teeth I heard, "*ALL THESE THINGS ARE GOING AWAY!*"

Meanwhile, my brother wrote a check to us to cover the towing and impound charges along with paying off a cash loan he took through us to get the vehicle in the first place. The towing expenses were paid along with the cash loan. A few days later, I was having my daily devotions with the Lord. I was basking in His presence and peace surrounded me. Suddenly, I was interrupted by my wife who had bad news. She had checked our bank account and it was -$500! My brother's check had bounced! I fought hard to keep the fear and anxiety at bay!

I finished my time with God, all the while trying to keep the stress, worry, and anxiety outside my mind. It was tough! It was also very difficult to find peace in God and His plans because my wife was having a tough time relaxing into that peace. Every time I would finally be at peace, it'd evaporate into thin air the moment my wife spoke something negative.

The original goal for this day was to get some grocery shopping done. Our son was in school, and we took our daughter to a babysitter with high hopes of making a successful shopping trip. The money situation weighed heavily on our shoulders though so we postponed the trip in order to deal with the situation. Our first stop was the bank. They didn't have the greatest news for us telling us that we would have to "just bite the bullet." We walked out to our vehicle, our heads hung low. We were broken and in desperate need of God. As we buckled, we looked straight ahead to see a bumper sticker that said, "More Jesus." I got the feeling that God was trying to get something across to us. Our next plan was to get a cash loan in hopes of putting the mess a few days ahead of us until we figured out the right course of action. The cash loan agency told me they couldn't do business with me at the time due to a payoff agreement I had with another company. I walked to my car feeling defeated once again but as we were driving out of the lot we saw another bumper sticker that was in the shape of a cross with the word, "Faith", in the center. We stopped and prayed that God would give us the strength that we needed to get through the day. As we finally made it to the store, I caught a glimpse of an old Christian friend that I had barely even had the chance of catching up with because not only did I lose his number each time he gave it to me, but also our schedules were so different. I knew in my heart that I was to go make conversation with him. As me and my wife spoke with him and his wife, I could feel strength begin to fill me once again. We all gathered in prayer and exchanged numbers once again and then we were off, filled with the joy of the Holy Spirit!

The cash loan thing eventually worked out and as I was depositing the money into my bank account, I heard the teller ask another gentleman how his day was going. He told the teller that he was having a horrible day because he just found out that he would need surgery both in his knees and back. I felt a nudge from the Holy Spirit. I finished my business with the bank and then stood off to the side as I waited for the man to finish up. Lies of the enemy started to swirl in my mind and fear tried to grip my heart. But with all that me and my wife had been going through, I decided that I had enough and that I was going to listen and obey what God was putting on my heart to do. I followed the man into the parking lot and said, "*Hey sir!*" He turned to face me, probably three times my size! "*Hey, I'm a*

Christian and I overheard your situation, would you mind if I prayed with you?" He squared up on me and looked me right in the eyes, throwing up his hands and bellowing, *"I don't have time for that!"* He angrily walked away. For a minute, I could not understand why the Lord would lead me to a man just to be rejected. I felt like the man had physically punched me right in the gut. The enemy said something in my mind like, *"See, if you share the Gospel, your just gonna keep getting hurt! Your gonna keep getting rejected!"* But then, as I thought about the situation, I felt the Holy Spirit rest on me and concluded that I'd rather be rejected repeatedly, rather than be separated from the love of my God. I struggled with so much rejection in my past that this should have been the nail in my coffin. But instead, it was such a healing reward and so worth it to be rejected! I started agreeing with God in the situation that the earth was not my home. It felt good. Something that should have hurt me, actually helped heal me. I was done caring what the world thought of me and I was done listening to the lies of the enemy!

It turns out that it was the day that I was
meeting with the pastor again to do some
counseling. I had no clue what today's topic
would pertain to, I just knew that worry tried to
chase me all the way there.

When I arrived, we dove right into it. The
pastor asked me, "*So how's everything been
going?*" "*Not good.*", I told him. And then I
unleashed all my financial difficulties upon him.
He instantly realized what I was going through
because he was going through a time of financial
testing himself. And then we started talking about
abiding in Christ's love. My pastor told me of
when Jesus said in the Bible, "*As the Father has
loved me, so have I loved you. Now remain in
my love.*" We discussed how no matter what the
world throws our way we are to abide in that
love, the love that only Jesus can give to us. And
then something clicked within me. I realized that
I had been believing the lies of the enemy and
not even knowing it! All my problems that I
couldn't figure out about myself were actually
lies! I always wondered why when I came to the

Lord, I felt completely free and at peace, but as
time went on, I drifted into depression as my fire
dimmed. I was believing the lies of the enemy
about myself all this time!

God hadn't allowed the enemy to sweep into
me, I had the Holy Spirit! The devil tricked me
into thinking that all these things were wrong with
me! They weren't! Yes, I needed more healing in
my life, but the Lord isn't into regression! He's
about moving forward! All about it! The moment
I realized this I walked back into my freedom.
Peace was mine for the taking only if I accepted
it.

Peace is also yours for the taking but only if
you accept it. The world is going to constantly try
to sabotage your peace with God with endless
assaults of stress, worry, and anxiety. It will

continue until our Lord's return, I can guarantee it! But there is one thing we can do to be safe from these heavy, soul sapping rains and that is to stand under the umbrella of Christ! Quit trying to make ends meet on and in your own terms. We as human beings are truly rascals. Jesus' burden is so light, yet lots of the time we think we can carry the burden of the world on our own shoulders, we can take care of our own problems. Friends, we cannot! If you are tired, come to Jesus. Are you tired of carrying that pit around in your stomach? You want to know what that pit is doing? It's like a cap on your well of living water! Unless removed, your river cannot flow to other people! That pit is blocking the power of the Spirit from flowing! It is time to get honest and press in with all your might into the mighty waters of the Living God! I've been where you are and am healing with you! You are not alone! Let go of your stress, worry and anxiety! Let in the peace of Christ and resist the lies of the enemy!

Come to me, all you who are weary and burdened, and I will give you rest. Take my yoke upon you and learn from me, for I am gentle and humble in heart, and you will find rest for your souls. For my yoke is easy and my burden is light.

MATTHEW 11:28-30

A FIRM FOUNDATION

I WAS PRAYING ALONE IN MY
BATHROOM.

It was in an act of surrender. Suddenly, I felt
Jesus put His hand on my head like He was
anointing me! It was strange yet wonderful! It
literally felt like a physical hand was touching my
forehead! I was reassured that He was indeed
with me!

The next day, my pastor called and asked if I
would be willing to speak a little bit next Sunday.
I agreed and then asked him if maybe we could
meet up for counseling again. (I was doing pretty
good, although I don't think you can ever get
enough counseling!) I was a little bit nervous
about speaking to the whole congregation but I
knew that the enemy was behind my

nervousness, and that the Lord had called me to speak.

✝

Opening up and being up front wasn't as difficult as it normally would have been to me. The pastor was like a brother to me so things always pretty much flowed naturally between us, I could tell him anything. I was still kind of struggling with my identity in Christ, that and complete surrender. I know what it feels like to have complete peace in the Lord, but occasionally I still had a heavy burden deep within. My flesh wants to do its own thing and satisfy its own desires but my spirit craves to be close to God and burn with passion for Him. Paul says in Galatians, "*For the flesh desires what is contrary to the Spirit, and the Spirit what is contrary to the flesh. They are in conflict with each other, so that you are not to do whatever you want.*" I know exactly what he meant. Sometimes I get so close to God, then my heart tries to pull away like it has a mind of its own. What am I so afraid of? God will never hurt me! My mind and heart act like my enemies. I have

174

chosen God and He has chosen me! There is no going back! No compromise! I will pick up my cross and follow Christ! There is no other way!

At every new counseling session, my friend reinforced my spirit. At times, I am weak. I am not left to fend for myself though, my brother is right beside me. We talked for about an hour. Time slips by like water each time. We bring the darkness to light in my life, exposing the schemes of the devil, and what he is trying to accomplish in it. I had been struggling a lot with my thoughts lately. Thoughts of lust had been ripping through my mind. Thoughts I didn't want but was tempted to act on. Jesus provided a way out each time, the enemy's traps never worked because I keep resisting and submitting to God. My pastor told me how when thoughts like those come to him, he immediately thinks about the glory of God and what it'll be like to worship Him in person for eternity! Soon the attacks stop because they were only bringing him closer to the Lord! (Great strategy!)

✝

I had also been dealing with a lot of swinging emotions lately. My friend revealed how sometimes the Lord gives the gift for people to feel the emotions of people around them so that they know what to pray for. This made sense. Not only could I sense the different emotions around me but I could also sense angelic or demonic atmospheres. Pastor thought maybe the enemy was trying to flip the gift that God had given me in order for me to believe the lie that something was wrong with me. Everything began to make sense! Another strange phenomenon that I was experiencing was physical pain that came on in the spur of a moment. He recounted to me how one time his ears started ringing, for a second he thought something was going on with him but then realized that someone needed prayer for their ears. As soon as he mentioned this, sure enough, someone had ringing in their ears and as soon as he prayed for them, the ringing left both of them! Amazing! This began to make sense to me as well. I wasn't always being attacked, but the Lord was showing me what to pray for!

I was still experiencing a little anxiety and worry along with a dose of fear every once and a while and we came to the conclusion that these were just tactics to get me off guard and away from the presence and peace of the Lord. We prayed, (I felt more healing taking place, a strange sensation in my belly and tingling throughout my limbs), and then we ended the session, joy overtaking both of us!

Maybe you're struggling yourself in these areas or maybe you just needed a little bit of encouragement. Jesus is so much stronger! Nothing can hold us back. NOTHING! I know there is no such thing as a perfect Christian. At one time in my life I thought there was but the truth is there is not! Christians are still human beings. We still struggle, sometimes a lot more than others. The only difference is that we know that we need help from our God and we're not afraid to ask for help. I need help! You need help! We all need help! We are weak! There is nothing wrong with admitting that, in fact there is strength in honesty. I'm not afraid to admit that I am weak for when I am weak, then I am strong in Christ! The moment when you begin to believe the lie that you are invincible and that you never need help is when you should begin to worry. Embrace your weakness with me! We need You, Lord Jesus! Come!

But he said to me, "My grace is sufficient for you, for my power is made perfect in weakness.".

2 CORINTHIANS 12:9

WHISPER IN MY HEART

I GOT AHOLD OF MY PASTOR FOR ANOTHER COUNSELING SESSION. THE PROBLEM WAS, HE ALREADY HAD PLANS THAT WEDNESDAY.

That Wednesday, we were all going to meet to do some work on the new "Prayer Room." That was the plan. Pastor felt in his spirit though that the time wasn't right so we rescheduled Wednesday as a day to talk. To be honest, I was a little relieved because I felt like I needed one more session to complete this section of the book. After the session, I realized how true this this really was!

†

Throughout the week prior to this session, I could increasingly hear the Lord speaking to me more clearly.

179

✝

I do a small lawn care service on the side. I had just gotten out of my store job and I was pretty exhausted. (That day had been truck unloading day. Picture a semi-trailer filled to the brim with big appliances!) That day also happened to be the day I did yard work for one of my clients.

✝

My sunglasses had been missing for weeks. In frustration, I said to myself, "*I really wish I had my sunglasses!*" To my surprise, I heard a still small voice answer me back, "*They are in your son's room!*" Immediately, I acted upon the new-found information. Once I got to my son's room though, I started to doubt if I had really heard the voice of God. There was only one way to find out though! (I knew if they were anywhere in my son's room, then they'd probably be under his bed!) I began shuffling and pulling out miscellaneous boxes and containers. Sure

enough, way in the back, there lay my sunglasses!
I felt the Holy Spirit rush through me as I
realized how tender God's love was for me, that
he'd even speak to me about the little things! I
fell even more in love with Him that afternoon!

To open up our session, this was one of the
first topics I told him about. Afterwards, we got
into talking about trusting God because I really
felt like this was one area that I needed to work
on. (The day prior, when thinking about my trust
with the Lord, the scripture Proverbs 3:5 kept
going through my heart and mind as a remedy,
*"Trust in the Lord with all your heart and lean
not on your own understanding."*) After hearing
what my pastor had to say, my insight began to
grow and I began to have more confidence in
trusting the Lord. We also talked about spiritual
gifts and how to use them. The biggest healing,
I'd have to say, wouldn't necessarily have been
the counseling this day though. I'd have to say it
was my ride home!

✝

I was driving on the freeway, when suddenly, a bald eagle appears and flies right across my field of vision! (I think I swerved a little trying to take in its majesty! To me, it represented, "Freedom.") Then I heard that same small whisper in my heart again, "*Take your wife on a date.*" I'm thinking to myself, "*I sure in the heck can't afford a date right now!*", but that thought was met with, "*It's on Me!*" And it was settled! My Daddy was paying for our date! Who was I to refuse His offer?

I got home and relayed the sudden change of plans to my wife. Money was tight, so we started bickering. I got angry and just wanted to say, "*Forget it then!*", but chose wisely to hold my tongue, press forward, and have patience. It paid off as God's plan molded together. We got a baby sitter., I chose a sappy romance that I knew my wife would like at the movies. It was actually

182

quite good I must say! I picked out one of my
wife's favorite restaurants. There was nothing
more to do than to sit back, trust God, and enjoy
each other's company as we took the 45-minute
drive to Traverse City. I wasn't settling for the
average hometown date. I was going all out for
my beautiful bride!

   We arrived at our destination and then
suddenly, a tidal wave of freedom hits me
seemingly out of nowhere! I'm no longer self-
conscious. I'm back to my goofy self! I'm
dancing like John Travolta in *Saturday Night
Fever*! I'm cracking my wife up like I'm Vegas's
number one comedian! It was truly something
special I must tell you! Best date I've been on,
hands down!

I can recall replacing all the lies of the enemy with the truths of God and standing firm in who God really created me to be. I didn't care what others thought of me or how they viewed me! That, my brothers and sisters, is the freedom that we have in Christ! We were made to be care free! Stop caring or worrying if you're not living up to the world's status quo. YOU.......
WERE....... NOT....... MEANT......TO!

Therefore I tell you, do not worry about your life, what you will eat or drink; or about your body, what you will wear. Is not life more than food, and the body more than clothes? Look at the birds of the air; they do not sow or reap or store away in barns, and yet your heavenly Father feeds them. Are you not much more valuable than they? Can any one of you by worrying add a single hour to your life?

MATTHEW 6:25-26

POOL PARTY

I BELIEVE WRITING THIS HAS BEEN A
FORM OF THERAPY FOR ME.

God truly works in amazing ways! (I know I've
already said that so many times throughout this
book but it is so true!) Many have asked me how
my relationship with my father is now that I am
an adult. I can't say that it's perfect but I can say a
lot of healing has taken place!

When I first gave my heart to the Lord, I
remember being so hungry and thirsty for His
truth! I was in church on Father's Day and the
pastor was preaching on honoring your father no
matter what he ever did to you. He spoke on
how doing so honored the Lord. I remember
feeling the Holy Spirit surge up inside me,

convicting my heart that what the pastor was
saying was indeed true.

   After service, I drove to my mother's house
where my father was having his morning coffee. I
sat down and told him I forgave him. You could
tell it hit him hard as tears welled up in his eyes.

   After that morning, I began to show him
respect by actually having civilized conversations
with him which had been so hard for me in the
past. Sometimes I'd go to work with him to make
a little extra money, and I'd find myself enjoying
my time with him. As a few years went by, I
forgot about honoring him. It seemed whenever
he was around it would greatly annoy me. I
always referred to him by his first name and I
could never tell him I loved him or hug him. As
time went on though I managed to get a few hugs

in when saying good bye and even told him I loved him a few times. In my flesh it was so awkward, but in my spirit, I felt healing and I knew God was smiling!

God showed me a new perspective with my dad. He showed me that hurt people hurt people and that a generational cycle had been going on in my family. He showed me that with His help, I'd be the one to end it!

My father opened up to me about getting abused by his stepdad. He told me how he'd be hit and called names in front of his other siblings. This led to a hatred of his stepfather and siblings.

As a child, I remember him playing a song by a guy named Charlie Rich called, *The Most Beautiful Girl.* The lyrics would go, *"Hey, did you happen to see the most beautiful girl in the world? And if you did, was she crying, crying? Hey, if you happen to see the most beautiful girl that walked out on me. Tell her, "I'm sorry.", tell her, "I need my baby", oh, won't you tell her that I love her."* He'd cry and tell us how he got married to a woman in Vietnam. He gave her all his combat pay and waited about nine days for her to show up at the airport. She never did. Now, thinking about this memory, I can see the pain he endured. Just hearing the song again brings back deep emotions as I picture tears running down my father's face. He had a hard life! The court documents show that he was diagnosed with Schizophrenia! What a hard life my father had been dealt! I never cared to view him as one of God's own children but a monster. I never cared before. I don't want my father to die though with unresolved issues. I want and greatly accept God's healing in our lives. I know it wasn't pretty growing up, but I can see God's hand in all of it. I truly forgive my father. I don't hold anything against him. I want the best for him and I want him to make it to Heaven.

Last Father's Day was a huge healing milestone for us. One of my brothers mentioned something about an outing with our father but then the idea faded. As Father's Day approached though, I had a strong urge to plan the day. I wanted it to be all my brothers and my dad fishing. I spoke to my father about it and it seemed like he always had an excuse not to go. Well, finally when the day approached, he agreed to it. In my head, I envisioned us all on a boat. But instead we decided to go to a pier right on Lake Michigan.

Only one of my brothers rode with me. We followed the overly annoying voice of our GPS to our destination. It was a beautiful sunny day. Even though we were still in Michigan, the warm sandy beach reminded me of Florida. People were lounging, flying kites, and fishing. It was

beautiful and the perfect place to start our
relationships all over again!

Our father arrived and it was a little awkward at
first, but then I began to feel like a child again
and like I actually had a real father. All my
brothers and I giddily talked with our father, like
kids trying to be the first to get his attention.
(This was the first time that we were actually all
together in the same place at the same time!)
Even though we never ended up catching
anything, it was one of the most enjoyable
experiences I had ever had with my father.
Afterwards we all sat down for a picnic. I knew
for sure God was restoring our broken family
unit!

Lately, I've felt even more of an urge to honor
my father. Sometimes, it's just so easy to revert

back to rebelliousness and bitterness towards my father but that is only in my flesh. My spirit wants to honor him and take care of him no matter how he treated me in the past. It's when I get closer to God that I get closer to my father.

I remember as a child, my father would always say, "*I take care of you now, but one day will you take care of me?*" I'd always agree. I see that coming to pass now. God's love is so much more powerful than unforgiveness and past resentment!

A few months back, we moved into a bigger apartment. Our old one only had two bedrooms, so with a son and a daughter, that wasn't really the best fit for us. After a year or more, we finally received a three bedroom. (I think at the time, it was more exciting for my wife than it was for me because I utterly detest moving!) This new apartment came with extra space, an extra bathroom a bigger kitchen, plus to my delight, a much larger basement! I've always felt like I needed my own little spot to call my own since going through the foster care system. I never had my own space then so it seems I crave it now to make up for it. Anyways, I threw a dartboard up, set up a mini pool table, replaced all the lightbulbs with cool stainless glass ones. I have my own writing station, a spot for my tools, a work area, as well as my prayer tent. I don't know if it sounds like much, but to me, this is my very own *Fortress of Solitude.*

I got the idea one day to show the space to my father. I invited him to play pool with me and ever since, every Saturday night is father and son pool time. Sometimes it's awkward, I'll admit. At times, it's hard to make eye contact with him but it seems like each Saturday a little more healing takes place. A healthy relationship is starting to blossom.

✝

The Lord never ceases to amaze me. As a child growing up, hate for my father flowed like venom through my veins. I never once thought I would ever talk to him again. I never wanted anything to do with him. The thought of him evoked feelings of fear and anger. It's so hard to comprehend the way God heals. I don't fully understand it all. How can I respect a man who never respected me? Only through the love and forgiveness of Christ! I want to encourage you to pursue forgiveness. Forgiveness is so freeing! It's inhuman to carry around bitterness. After all we were made to love! Once you begin to realize that hurt people hurt people, then your eyes will be opened to what started the chain reaction in the first place and it all leads back to the Garden of Eden!

Let God transform you inwardly by a complete change of your mind. Then you will be able to know the will of God, what is good and is pleasing to him and is perfect.

ROMANS 12:2

193

PART III REVELATIONS

FEAR OF MAN

As a result of my endless rejections, I opened up the door to demonic fear.

I didn't want fear to come and reside with me where ever I went! My mind often goes crazy with absurd ideas! In reality, most people around me aren't even paying attention to me, nor do they care to. But to me, when I step in a store, all eyes are on me and I'm immediately being judged and rejected by every single one of them! It's crazy!

Just last weekend, we were getting ready to close the store where I work for the night. A couple came walking in to pick up a washer and dryer. As soon as they entered the doors, the atmosphere just shifted into chaos! My mouth became dry as the desert and when I tried to talk I began to stutter. They began to argue with my co-worker and I knew in my head it was going to be a long ride. Shakily, I walked back to get their stuff ready. Our doors read, "Employees Only", but they completely disregarded the sign and walked through the doors with their kids. I didn't know how to say that they couldn't be back there with me, but in my fear, I let it slide. The husband started yelling that his wife bought junk and an argument soon ensues. Afterwards, he went to get his vehicle to drive to the back-loading ramp and I was stuck with the wife and the kid's in an uncomfortable situation. Time seemed to stop. I felt like I was falling apart. Eventually, the husband got to the back. I tried to explain our procedures but he seemed to be drunk or high and wouldn't listen to anything I had to say. Demonic fear began to inflate me like a balloon. His tailgate wouldn't go down, so he says we'll just lift them over. Inside I'm panicking because I know that if any damage occurs to the expensive units, then I'll be held responsible. The wife comes out right as all of this is happening and her husband and she began to fight and scream at each other again. I'm stuck in the middle of it. Inside, I'm praying that God would take the consuming fear away. After the fight, the woman runs up to her new appliances

and starts screaming, "*Look at those dents!
Those were never there before! Oh, my God!
What did you do!*" I stand there dumbstruck
knowing that these were closeout units and that
was probably the reason why they had the small
dents. After this uncomfortable situation, the
irate women went inside and starts arguing with
my employee. I try to explain that the washer and
dryer need to be placed in the back of their
pickup a certain way or else they will fly out. The
husband says, "*I don't care if they fly out! Let
them!*" The man is being so stubborn that I allow
him to have his way.

As we go back inside, his wife is arguing with
my co-worker over the price of a vacuum. Next
the husband gets involved. They give up on the
vacuum and move on to a damaged grill that we
can't sell. It seems as if the chaos will never end.
But it does. We close and I'm still shaking and
my heart is beating a thousand miles an hour!

I head to the store, and the feeling of fear still follows me. It's a while before I can shake it. I continue to pray in my head that God would take the fear away. I try to avoid direct eye contact with people and swear I can hear some of them making light of me. Finally, once I return home, a few hours later, the fear disappears.

To be honest, even when I see a group of teens I get extremely nervous. Subconsciously, yet again, worst case scenarios flash through my mind. I shy away from large groups in fear of rejection. Rejection is scarier than death itself for me.

†

This circus has been going on since I was just a little boy. But God wants to bring me out of this craziness! His desire isn't for me or anyone else to be tortured like this. This is so unnatural! It's all just one big lie, it's foundation, fear! And fear must go right now in the name of Jesus! God doesn't want to wait till you enter His pearly gates to give you the life you've always dreamed of! He wants to give you your dream right now! Right this instant as your reading these words! Your dream of complete peace and serenity is a breath away if only you'll accept Him to protect you, not that fear!

Take a stance with me right now, no more walls! Let's refuse to let anything separate us from the Lord our God! Fear will never protect us, it only holds us captive and tortures us. No more inner walls. Let the peace of Jesus flow through and crumble them.

There is no fear in love. But perfect love drives out fear, because fear has to do with punishment. The one who fears is not mad perfect in love.

I JOHN 4:18

INSUFFICIENT LOVE

W HEN GOD CREATED THE FAMILY
UNIT, HE MADE IT SO THAT EACH
GENERATION WOULD PASS DOWN
BLESSINGS, NOT CURSES.

Grandparents to parents and parents to their
children. The devil likes to get his claws in once
and a while and mess things up. Usually, if you
have a bad childhood, it is because your parents
did too. They didn't necessarily crave this for
you, they just didn't know any better. How can
they give you something that they have never
had? This is where compassion and forgiveness
come in. Truth be told, your parents most likely
lived a similar childhood to yours. They may
never tell you, but maybe their parents abused
them too.

As you go through life, you'll most likely try to fill the empty void, where love and nurturing should have been, with idols. I know I did myself. I few of my idols were video games, porn, drugs and alcohol, etc. You'll always feel that void your whole life unless you let God give you what you were missing as a child. He is the ultimate Father who understands that earthly parents mess up sometimes and He will more than willingly fill those needs right now for you if you choose to let Him in. This wasn't His plan! This isn't His fault! Let down your guard right now and soak in the love you never got as a child! Run to the arms of the Father and don't stop! Let Him hold you close! You are His child!

Whoever does not love does not know God, because God is love.

1 JOHN 4:8

LONELINESS

THINK OF THE VERY FIRST TIME IN
YOUR LIFE WHERE YOU FELT SAD.

It most likely was a very traumatic experience,
something or someone that hurt you. It most
likely opened the door to loneliness. In that
moment of time, when that experience took
place, loneliness snuck in and made itself home
in your heart. Maybe your whole life like me,
you've felt alone in a crowded place. Just now as I
write this, the Lord brought into my mind where
loneliness came in at. My father would often
burst into fits of rage and just scream at us. He
would tell us that we're not getting anything to eat
for the day, only bread and water. He would then
proceed to strip me and my brother of our
clothes and make us go to bed naked. I have no
clue what was going through his mind to make us
do such an odd task, but thinking upon it,
loneliness was so thick in that moment. I would
hide under my blankets in shame and just soak
in loneliness and worthlessness.

☦

Can we heal together right now? I know it hurts, I'm feeling it right now too, but we must expose and get rid of these negative emotions altogether! They can't alter our lives any longer, we must move on towards a brighter future! Embrace the pain and emotion these memories bring. It will only sting for a little. Receive forgiveness for allowing "loneliness" to enter. Forgive others, yourself, and God. Don't move on until you feel complete peace over the situation. Let the Healer heal you! The truth is, you're not alone and you never were! Even when it seemed like you were, God was always with you!

For the sake of his great name the Lord will not reject his people, because the Lord was pleased to make you his own.

1 SAMUEL 12:22

FREEDOM

WHEN YOU REALIZE GOD IS WITH YOU, FREEDOM WILL BEGIN TO MANIFEST IN YOUR MIND.

The freedom of Christ will flow through your veins and you'll take off and soar on the wings of eagles! You weren't meant to be caged! You were meant to be wild and free like the deer of the fields.

Freedom is worth dying for. So many of our brave men do it every day as soldiers on the front line. Our General, Jesus, knew the cost of freedom when He was nailed to the cross. Without the giving of one's life, there is no freedom! The same goes for us as soldiers of the Lord's army. We are called to die. Die to ourselves spiritually and if the need may be, even physically. Before freedom comes surrender.

The white flag of surrender ushers in freedom
like the warm spring air at the end of winter.
Complete surrender frees you from the cares and
the worries of this world, in turn, making you
available to the Kingdom of our Lord, King
Jesus, for His service. Become a humble servant
and you'll be freer than the dolphins in the ocean
or the wild horses of the west!

When I think of "freedom", I am reminded of
the end scene in *Braveheart* with Mel Gibson.
He had led a successful revolt against the English
armies but was eventually caught, imprisoned
and tortured. Right before they kill him publicly,
He screams, "*FREEDOM!*", at the top of his
lungs! It's so powerful! Jesus did the same thing
when He said, "*It is finished!*", before He died
on the cross. Your freedom was bought at a cost,
don't neglect it or take it for granted!

Now the Lord is the Spirit, and where the Spirit of the Lord
is, there is freedom.

2 CORINTHIANS 3:17

CHILDLIKENESS

Jᴇsᴜs sᴘᴏᴋᴇ ᴀʙᴏᴜᴛ ʙᴇɪɴɢ ʙᴏʀɴ ᴀɢᴀɪɴ
ᴀɴᴅ ʙᴇɪɴɢ ᴄʜɪʟᴅʟɪᴋᴇ.

He said we must become like children to enter
the Kingdom of Heaven. When I first gave my
heart to Him, He spoke something very simple
into my heart, "*If a child shouldn't do it, then
neither should you.*" It really made a lot of sense
to me and I believe it's a great guide to follow.
Always compare and see if a child would be
engaging in it. Would a child look at porn? No.
Would a child get drunk? No. Would a child
smoke cigarettes? No. Would a child watch an R
rated movie? No.

It might sound a little too dramatic but we're to
be pure and clean like Jesus was. I'm not saying
you can't have fun and must chastise yourself

severely. I'm saying that there is a way to have godly fun the way God intended you to. We are called to walk the same way that Jesus did when He was here on earth. We should be spitting images, pure and innocent before our Father. God said not to touch anything unclean and He will draw near to you. We are to separate from the world around us! I'm not saying be immature or anything of that nature, but become like a child because we who believe are all God's children!

Truly I tell you, unless you change and become like little children, you will never enter the kingdom of heaven!

MATTHEW 18:3

ONENESS WITH SPOUSE

Becoming one with your spouse is
a huge way to overcome rejection!

The Lord has led me through this process
throughout the last few days. I've come to realize
that the only acceptance you need in life is
God's, but after Him, your spouse. Who cares
what others think, your spouse obviously chose
you for a reason!

✝

They were made specifically for you to both
help and encourage you along life's journey! God
is so good! He said it isn't good for man to be
alone and He did something about it! He
designed your significant other especially for you,
a tailored fit! You may feel a wall and stress
keeping you from giving everything to your lover.
This wall needs to come down as well!

When me and my wife started dating, she asked me if I had ever had intimate relations with anyone else. I told her no out of fear of not being her one and only. This lie festered throughout our whole marriage, keeping us from the blessings that God had for us. Not only had I had an intimate relationship with someone else before I got with her, while dating, I was also unfaithful during the beginning of our marriage. I was tempted numerous times. Every single time I met with a girl, nothing would happen. I would try to be intimate with them but simply couldn't. God was protecting me the whole time! I still call it being "unfaithful" because I was willing to cheat on my girlfriend. It makes me smile now knowing that God blocked anything from happening every time!

I remember, I was new in the Lord and I started volunteering somewhere. There was a pretty girl who caught my attention and throughout my volunteering, I sensed a connection between the two of us. She started flirting with me. Someone donated witchcraft items so all the employees and I gathered around, fascinated. We found tarot cards. We started playing with them and it said that she would get pregnant. One of the guys said that I would be the one to impregnate her. After that, the flirting got worse and eventually led to us being alone and her asking me what I'd do if her pants dropped. I was shocked and snapped back to reality, leaving and severing my connection with her for good! The devil set so many traps along the way for me. He knew I had a lust problem!

There were various other encounters but I won't go into serious detail. Just know that situations arose where I could have been easily ensnared.

✝

The point is, I kept most of this stuff from my wife until the other night, I was taking a bath and somehow the conversation came up and I just spilled the beans! I couldn't hold my secrets any longer! And it was so freeing! It hurt her deep but to heal, I knew that I needed to be honest. The weird thing is that I never planned to tell her anything, EVER! But me and my wife continually pray for our marriage and the Lord has heard us! Now it's like we've been snapped back to when we first started dating! I have a crush on her again and we can be intimate on levels that I would never have thought to be possible! Something demonic lifted when I brought my shadows to the light!

It may feel like the sky will come tumbling down if you tell them, but this is the enemy trying to keep your secrets in the dark. I've heard it said before, you're only as sick as your secrets. Get rid of all secrets between you and your spouse and be ready for a marriage revival! It's not easy and it may hurt for a while but God can heal and take the bad memories away!

Though one may be overpowered, two can defend themselves. A cord of three strands is not quickly broken.

ECCLESIASTES 4:12

ACCEPTANCE

I STUMBLED INTO SIN.

I felt terrible. I felt like I had failed God and failed everyone around me. Yet it was in that moment that I realized how evil our human flesh is and how desperately we need God. In my flesh, I wanted to keep busy so as not to think about my failure but I felt a gentle nudge to talk to God. I got still and cried out to God telling Him how truly sorry I was. I didn't feel shamed but instead felt the love of a Father envelope me. It brought joy to my heart and made me leap. A waterfall of truth and encouragement came pouring out from the throne room of Heaven and on to me. In that moment, I realized how great of a purpose I have on this earth and how great the Father's love was for me! I would try to do hobbies around the house but my soul craved more intimacy, affection and love. It's contagious! My walls were down and I was soaking up my Daddy's love like a sponge in water. Listening to God's voice for me and ignoring what man has said about me, I began to swell with godly confidence to accomplish the very mission I was put on earth for, after all I am truly accepted by my Lord and Creator! I can do anything! So can you!

All those the Father gives me will come to me, and whoever comes to me I will never drive away.

JOHN 6:37

STILLNESS

W<small>E LIVE IN A FAST-PACED WORLD.</small>

Everywhere you look, people are zipping around
to and fro. In our culture, it's odd if you're not
busy. Busy with work, busy with school, busy on
your phone. And there's got to be noise in the
background wherever we might be. But it's very
essential to turn everything off and have quiet
time with God. Just you and Him. No
distractions. He will build you up in this
"quietness". Like an expert surgeon, He will
perform intricate surgery on you if you let Him.
It needs to be done! Let Him heal you! Become
vulnerable and trust your Creator. Though the
past wounds may hurt to bring to the surface, the
end result will be so worth it! This is part of
healing from rejection. It takes time, but soon,
once you stop caring about what others think and
only start caring about what your Savior thinks,
you'll be carefree. I'm still in the process but
He's showing me step by step so that I can help
others heal too. Jesus had that quiet time with
His Father every day and it made a world of

difference. We are to be reflections of Jesus. I watched a movie called "War Room". (Spoiler alert!) In the movie, a husband and wife were having some marriage problems. The wife was a real estate agent and happened to meet an old woman who was selling her house. As the older lady was showing her house, they stumbled across the lady's war room or "prayer closet." In it, she conquered her most intense battles through prayer. The younger woman then gets into the habit of prayer and restores her marriage. After seeing this film, it inspired me to make my own "War Room" in one of our walk-in closets at our apartment. It became an amazing way to escape and spend quiet time with the Lord. When we switched apartments, we didn't have a walk-in closet so I set up our tent in the basement and made it into a "prayer tent." (Hey, they kind of did the same thing in the Old Testament, just saying!) It's been a marvelous time growing in the Lord in my tent! That's my spot for quietness with my Lord. I encourage you to find a favorite spot to spend quiet time with God. Scripture says that Jesus would often withdraw to a quiet place in order to pray. Like I said if He did it, then so should we.

Very early in the morning, while it was still dark, Jesus got up, left the house and went off to a solitary place, where he prayed.

MARK 1:35

LOVE YOURSELF

I'M NOT SAYING BE SELF-OBSESSED.

I am saying just as a verse in Proverbs says, "*So a man thinks in his heart so he is.*" We've got to recognize the importance and uniqueness of our lives! God created you for a purpose! Your life has value! You're valuable beyond all the money in the world! God's got such great plans for you! All this is true but until you actually take hold of these truths and believe in them, you'll never be completely healed, you'll always have a deep hurt in your heart. Even as a believer, it's been difficult to love myself. I've been told so many hateful things in my life that I actually began to believe them. Until I start to believe what the Lord says about me, until I take down the wall that separates me from God, then I'll always have turmoil in my soul. How can we believe what God says about us? Because He is not a man that He should lie! He is the God of the whole universe; His foundation is truth! He loves you, therefore you should love yourself. Regardless of what people may have said in the past, your

Creator will never hurt you, He does not take pleasure in your pain. He's not sadistic. The enemy may have tricked you into thinking that He is but, truth be told, He is not! He loves you beyond words! He loves you beyond all the galaxies that He created! You are worthy to be loved! You are worthy to give love and you are worthy to receive love. Jesus made this very clear by dying on the cross for your sins! He didn't have to! It wasn't the nails that held Him on that cross, it was His love for you! Take some time to stare at your reflection in the mirror today. Notice the intricate details in your face. Realize how wonderfully and beautifully you were crafted. Those things that were said about you were only said to stop you in your tracks! They are lies! Everything that He has made is good, including you! He doesn't make mistakes! It's time to show yourself some love!

Love the Lord your God with all your heart and with all your soul and with all your mind and with all your strength. The second is this: 'Love your neighbor as yourself.' There is no commandment greater than these."

MARK 12:30-31

JOURNEY

M Y LIFE HASN'T BEEN ALL THAT
MAJESTIC, BUT A LONG-LIFE LESSON.

I praise God for all my sufferings now though!
All those things that happened in my life now
give my life meaning! Since I've went through so
many things myself, I can relate and help others
who went through the same situations as well! It's
so exciting when you find your purpose in life!
The enemy is just giving you ammunition to
glorify God! There's a lot of evil in the world but
we can make our lives count and be the good
that combats and wins victoriously over evil! In
fact, if Jesus is our Lord and Savior, we have
already won! Yay! Take on that mindset with me,
we have already won! As Jesus spoke, "It is
finished!", on the cross, it really became finished!
There still is a lot of guerilla warfare going on
because the devil and his demons are sore losers
but they have indeed lost!

All the rejection, hurt, and torments that you have faced will all be worth it someday! When we finally enter our "promised land", the Lord will show us His perspective on our past lives and we will see what really was happening in the spiritual. I believe we don't see and know all we are affecting at the time because God is protecting us from the pride that could ensnare us and trip us up in our journey here on earth. We need to stay humble at the feet of Jesus!

Think back with me of all the bad things that have happened in your life that have left you feeling "wrecked". The enemy thought he was winning and maybe in the moment he was, but now envision with me the testimony of where you came from and where you are now! One of my all-time favorite scriptures I believe would have to be Revelation 12:11, "*They overcame him by the blood of the Lamb and by the word of their testimonies.*" Wow! What a statement! We overcome the devil through our Savior's sacrifice

and through the testimony that He gives us! Even
though many people of the world have their
spiritual eyes and ears closed to the Gospel, they
are definitely gonna notice something different
about you! Something strange and wonderful!
God will use your circumstances to make others
curious about Him! Release and surrender to
His peace and He will effortlessly guide your life
in the right direction!

    I recently felt led to leave my job and to step
out into full time ministry. This is a somewhat
scary idea for me since I am raising a family. I
was obedient to what I felt the Lord put in my
heart though. My last day of work, various
appliances started shaking by themselves
throughout our store. My co-worker believed
there were ghosts in the store. I felt like Satan
was shaking in anger that I was about to step into
my destiny. My wife said he was shaking in fear!
The day was pretty much chaotic but my last
customers really confirmed God's plan for my
life. We got into conversation about my life and
what I felt called to do. Right as they were

heading out the door, the wife says to me, "*It doesn't matter what anybody says about you, you're already a success! The Man upstairs has big plans for your life!*" As my last customers headed out the door, my last day ended with a confirmation that I was really doing what the Lord wanted me to do. Please keep me and my family in your prayers as we step out in faith and obedience to what the Lord has called us to do!

However, I consider my life worth nothing to me; my only aim is to finish the race and complete the task the Lord Jesus has given me-the task of testifying to the good news of God's grace.

ACTS 20:24

"IF YOU LIVE FOR PEOPLE'S ACCEPTANCE, YOU WILL DIE FROM THEIR REJECTION."

-LECRAE

ABOUT THE AUTHOR

Ethan Hunt is the loving father of two, Marshall and Arianna. He is married to his High School sweetheart, Christine. Ethan is extremely family oriented. He strives hard to produce a home life that he never experienced as a child. He is a firm, Spirit-filled believer. His aim is not to cling to a religion but to a relationship with his true Father. His ministry, *Christ is Risen Ministries*, exerts itself to find anyone who will listen and to share the Good News with them. He's training in the art of motivational speaking in order to help encourage anyone else who has ever been through hardships in their lives and to let them know that there is a hope that is only found at the foot of the cross. He is determined to live his whole life for Christ, no matter what, and he can't wait for the day when eternity crashes with the present!

THE CAGELESS MOVEMENT

The Cageless Movement is an idea that I came up with as a platform to reach other people. I realize that everyone goes through their own times and at times are locked in invisible cages of their own. My goal is to set people free! My plan is to start a movement that reaches both the young and the old. Flowing through schools to jails to churches, anywhere or any place that will hear what I have to say. This is a cause that is very near and dear to my heart. I know it is what I was put on earth to do. I want to be the "resistance" that goes against the grain of society, that says, "No!" to moral decay and "Yes!", to spiritual freedom! I want to start a movement because I know what it's like to be stuck in a cage! I know the claustrophobic fear that envelopes! I know the pain and suffering! I have lived it! Now in return for being set free myself, I owe it to my brothers and sisters around the world to set them free as well. For we weren't made to live in a cage but to live wild and free!

HIRING INFORMATION

Ethan is available for hire for either speaking engagements or for personal book writing lessons. He's also in search of a publisher. For further information, or if you'd like to contact Ethan, please visit, thecagelessmovent.com.

Made in the USA
Middletown, DE
05 January 2023

17936971R00151